P9-BIC-493

Teach MORE and Discipline Less

Teach MORE and Discipline Less

Barbara Reider

Preventing Problem Behaviors in the K-6 Classroom

CORWIN PRESS
A Sage Publications Company
Thousand Oaks, California

Copyright © 2005 by Corwin Press.

All rights reserved. When forms and sample documents are included, their use is authorized only by educators, local school sites, and/or noncommercial entities who have purchased the book. Except for that usage, no part of this book may be reproduced or utilized in any form or by any means, electronic or mechanical, including photocopying, recording, or by any information storage and retrieval system, without permission in writing from the publisher.

For information:

Corwin Press
A Sage Publications Company
2455 Teller Road
Thousand Oaks, California 91320
www.corwinpress.com

Sage Publications Ltd.
1 Oliver's Yard
55 City Road
London EC1Y 1SP
United Kingdom

Sage Publications India Pvt. Ltd.
B-42, Panchsheel Enclave
Post Box 4109
New Delhi 110 017 India

Printed in the United States of America.

Library of Congress Cataloging-in-Publication Data

Reider, Barbara.
Teach more and discipline less: Preventing problem behaviors in the K-6 classroom / Barbara Reider.
        p. cm.
Includes bibliographical references and index.
ISBN 0-7619-8892-0 (cloth)—ISBN 0-7619-8893-9 (pbk.)
    1. Classroom management. 2. Elementary school teaching. I. Title.
LB3011.R39 2005
371.102′4—dc22

                                2004016461

04 05 06 07 10 9 8 7 6 5 4 3 2 1

Acquisitions Editor:	Kylee Liegl
Editorial Assistant:	Jaime Cuvier
Production Editor:	Melanie Birdsall
Copy Editor:	Patricia Oman, Publication Services, Inc.
Typesetter:	C&M Digitals (P) Ltd.
Proofreader:	Kris Bergstad
Indexer:	Michael Ferreira
Cover Designer:	Tracy E. Miller

Contents

Preface

A Focus on Prevention

Many teaching problems will be solved in the next few decades. There will be new learning environments and new means of instruction. One function, however, will always remain with the teacher: to create the emotional climate for learning. No machine, sophisticated as it may be, can do this job.

—Haim Ginott, 1942
Teacher and Child

Good teachers can prevent discipline problems by developing effective classroom management skills. In fact, the best teachers spend very little time dealing with student misbehavior. It's not that they ignore it, but they have established strategies for preventing problems in the first place. With a focus on prevention, these teachers organize and maintain an environment in which students feel secure, happy, and challenged . . . kid-successful classrooms.

Over the years I have benefited from observing many highly effective teachers in their classrooms, not only in California where I teach, but in other states as well as in Europe. From these exemplary teachers I have gathered many time-tested ideas, techniques, and strategies to include in the pages of this book.

Perhaps you too have had the good fortune to watch expert teachers in action. If so, you have undoubtedly taken note of the class climate, the

AUTHOR'S NOTE: For the purpose of fluency, the masculine form of the pronoun will be used throughout this book in the traditional way.

"feeling in the air" within successful classrooms. It is a feeling of warmth and caring beneath the expectations, of calmness underlying the enthusiasm. In these classrooms children know it is safe to risk, safe to make mistakes, safe even to fail. In these classrooms children can most effectively learn.

But such a beneficial atmosphere doesn't just fall into place. It must be created, consciously and deliberately, by a teacher possessing (1) essential skills and (2) attributes of acceptance and caring. Such a teacher cares enough to delve beneath telltale misbehavior and reach a child who is failing. Such a teacher realizes the vital importance of an effective learning climate and is skillful enough to become a master of classroom management.

Classroom management, a main focus of this book, refers to all things that teachers do to organize their time, their students, their curriculum, and their materials. It is, to most knowledgeable educators, a prerequisite; it is "what has to come first" in the classroom so that learning can take place and discipline problems can be averted.

The nation's teachers possess a wide diversity of management skills. These skills directly contribute to an equally wide diversity of successful and unsuccessful schools. And schools have a tough enough time these days. Challenges faced by educators include the growing prevalence of rudeness, negative attitudes, lack of parental support, and even violence. Many of today's students enter our classrooms lacking values of respect and responsibility; many struggle with success-hindering low self-esteem. All such issues make it difficult for teachers to remain positive and effective.

However, this book proclaims an unfailing faith in the everyday hard-working classroom teacher, earnestly open to new ideas and insights. Every teacher can become a better classroom manager. You may be searching for a few workable ideas to sharpen your teaching skills. Or you may be one of many who admit that discipline is a priority that permeates the very air of your classroom with its constant challenges. Perhaps you find yourself asking, "What can I do so I can teach more and discipline less?" You're in the boat with lots of company, all searching for methods by which we can avoid the role of disciplinarian. We all need the specific skills to deal effectively and humanely with the small irritations, the daily conflicts, and the sudden crises.

Supporting its focus on discipline prevention by setting up the environment, this book will help you

- Recognize causes of misbehavior
- Tender clear limits and logical consequences
- Build rapport and cooperation
- Raise the level of student responsibility
- Find alternatives for rewards and punishment

Good teachers can remember the day they stepped into their very first classrooms. Since that day they have developed, tested, and refined their craft until it worked for them. These teachers will tell you they never stop learning. All teachers can learn basic techniques of understanding misbehavior and improving classroom management. All teachers can meet today's challenges one child at a time!

Note to the New Guys

Welcome to the profession. You have now jumped in head-first, ready or not, to the whole new world of teaching. And chances are, you're going to love it!

You'll love the people who run the school . . . the secretaries and custodians! Get on their good side . . . they can be immeasurably helpful.

You'll love the teachers, especially those with ready smiles. Do a lot of listening. . . . You'll be surprised at the little tips you'll hear inadvertently, such as who to approach for a new pencil sharpener and where to find the hidden stash of chocolate.

You'll love the kids . . . the quick learners and the math whizzes, the whiners and the blamers, the cute clever ones and the mama's boys, the smilers and the pleasers, the bullies and the braggarts.

You'll love the chance, at last, to use your creativity: to invent new science experiments, to bring to life the great masters of literature, to direct plays, to inspire young poets, to set out the art materials and just watch the kids create!

You are now one of us . . . hoping and striving for the best in every day, determined and intuitively caring and having fun! Now it's time for you, too, to tune into that beautiful artistry for teaching that's inside of you!

Make every day a good one!

Acknowledgments

It is a paradox that although some teachers are clearly masters of classroom management, they cannot readily explain what it is they do or how they do it. Usually soft-spoken and unpretentious, these experts nevertheless have "in their little fingers" the ability to quell a classroom full of potential firecrackers and deliver a lesson effectively.

I set out to interview several of these teachers in order to conduct research for this book and found myself in the company of some exemplary educators. To them I owe my gratitude. They include Arlene Barooshian, Barbara Heglie, Mary McKeown, and Judy McClurg, from whom I cajoled secrets of handling the younger kids in school. From Doug Bush, Corinne Gulas, and Cynthia Lowery I pulled techniques for working with the older crew. My deepest thanks goes to them for sharing their wisdom.

Other educators and friends from far and near freely shared their insights and suggestions along with their encouragement, and Kathy Landis shared her expertise as an editor. To all of them I owe my heartfelt appreciation. And loving thanks goes to my husband, Jim, for his never-ending optimism and support.

PUBLISHER'S ACKNOWLEDGMENTS

Corwin Press gratefully acknowledges the contributions of the following reviewers:

Jacie Bejster
Classroom Teacher
Fort Pitt Elementary School
Pittsburgh, PA

Greg Elder
Teacher-Librarian
Evergreen Middle School
Everett, WA

Leslie Keiler
Assistant Professor
Department of Education
University of Richmond
Richmond, VA

Sonia Trehan
Head Start Classroom Teacher
Potomac High School
Oxon Hill, MD

T. J. Williams
Fifth-Grade Teacher
Bethel Elementary School
Greenville, SC

About the Author

Barbara Reider has been a dedicated educator for over 30 years, gaining a multitude of experience in classroom management and continually striving to capture the many motivations that drive behavior.

She is the author of two previous books for teachers and parents: *A Hooray Kind of Kid: A Child's Self-Esteem and How to Build It* and *Notes in the Lunchbox: How to Help Your Child Succeed at School.* A motivating speaker for numerous school districts, education conferences, and parent groups, she has presented workshops throughout the country. In addition, Barbara has conducted seven annual speaking tours for educators in Denmark.

Noted for her interest in her fellow teachers and their empowerment, Barbara has produced a video, *Building Confident Kids*, for use in staff development programs throughout the United States and Canada. Her books and videos are also published and produced in Denmark.

She is a child advocate who has dedicated her professional career to helping children who are failing, either academically or socially, and to improving classroom management skills in teachers. Barbara transforms theory into workable techniques, bringing information, inspiration, and humor to her readers.

1 Set Yourself Up for Success

DELIVERING AN UNEQUIVOCAL MESSAGE

It's Monday morning. The school day is beginning, outside your door. Students arrive and begin to line up, everyone is talking, and various moods can be observed, from excitement to dreaminess. The students know they are free to visit with friends, and they seem happy to be there.

Then you arrive, greeting them with a big smile. You are fully aware that this is the time and the place, outside the door, where you will deliver by your very demeanor a most essential message. Without words, your appearance and your expression will say, "The teacher is in charge here and happy to see you. As we enter the classroom, our attitude is one of mutual respect. Together we will make this classroom a good place in which to learn."

The message is unequivocal though unspoken, yet delivered in a friendly way. The positive comments that you subsequently make will reinforce the message and will also reiterate how much you care for them: "Good morning! I'm glad to see you looking so bright and splendid today!" You brief them with a few plans: "This morning we have two teams ready for our spelling relay, and computer lab at 11:00. And I do believe it's Kevin's birthday!"

Today is a new day, a fresh start. As the students file into the room, your no-nonsense demeanor and your words remind them that the rules and standards for their classroom are now in effect. You are confident that your groundwork of classroom management has been reinforced.

School has begun, outside the door.

SURVIVAL SKILL NUMBER 1: CLASSROOM MANAGEMENT

Teaching is a rewarding but undoubtedly challenging endeavor. Perhaps you are a new teacher fresh out of college, perhaps you're changing to a new grade level, or maybe you are an experienced educator gathering new and different ideas. Whatever your level of experience, teaching will have its challenges, and managing a classroom must come first.

Classroom management is survival skill number 1, and it begins with a "certain presence" that subtly demands respect. This presence is an attitude or manner found in effective teachers, whether new to the profession or experienced, whether young or old. It is an attitude that greatly aids their ability to manage a group of students with seemingly very little effort.

A "certain presence" is hard to define, but may be described by the laudatory remark of a fellow teacher. "Mrs. J. just has those kids in the palm of her hand every minute of the day," she comments. "I don't know how she does it."

However, if we look closely at the behavior of an effective classroom manager, we will most likely find that he or she

- Remains calm in all circumstances
- Smiles a lot
- Speaks with a quiet voice
- Is attentive to each individual child
- Remains focused
- Obviously has established rules with students
- Remains courteous in the face of anger
- Maintains a positive attitude

Mastering classroom management, survival skill number 1, is not just for beginners. Every teacher, green as a cucumber or wrinkled as a prune, must continually work to improve the strategies of managing a classroom. We all strive to develop and refine the techniques which bring us success, and this refinement continues throughout our careers.

The Message Is:

The teacher who has mastered classroom management knows that a delicate but crucial balance must be found, a balance between being an authority figure and being a buddy. The master teacher reaches for this balance with every encounter, delivers it with assurance, and strives to maintain it throughout the day.

Figure 1.1   The teaching day begins outside the door.

KIDS DON'T CARE HOW MUCH YOU KNOW UNTIL THEY KNOW HOW MUCH YOU CARE

A teacher who greets her class with assurance and a smile every day knows that teachers teach more by who they are than what they say. She realizes it's important to make sure that a message of caring comes through along with the respect she engenders. She is consciously and purposefully cheerful when she speaks with her children.

When Mrs. McKeown welcomes the children in her class each morning, she makes it a point to say their names, and to ask a quick question here and there. "How did the soccer game go, Billy?" "How was the party, Birthday Girl?"

Being a caring teacher means remembering details about students' lives. It means writing notes to students, a little thank-you for the gifts they make or bring you, or an acknowledgement of a thoughtfulness that you observed. Being a caring teacher means asking students what they think, and then caring about the answers. It means responding authentically and respectfully rather than giving patronizing pats on the head. And it includes being available, as time permits, for private conversations on kid-relevant issues.

A teacher like Mary McKeown is very cognizant that her caring and respectful manner eases her task of classroom management. She realizes that when she listens patiently, apologizes for something she has said, or shows concern for others, she is setting herself up as a model, showing the students how to conduct themselves in the classroom.

Teachers need to encourage children to care about themselves and each other. Caring children rarely disrupt classroom activities, have conflict with peers, or bully others. Teachers thereby play a role in nurturing the social and emotional development of their children along with their intellectual growth. By dedicating themselves as role models, teachers find that their actions, attitudes, and expectations greatly influence how children act.

Educators fully realize the importance of modeling positive behavior. They know that students will succeed in school and score higher on standardized tests if they spend their day in a positive learning environment. It is the caring teachers who model the behaviors which will create that climate.

Mrs. McKeown holds sacred her opportunity to be a role model, with a successful mixture of kindness and humor conducted in a businesslike, task-oriented atmosphere. She shows the way for her children to follow, stressing cooperation, respect, and fairness for all.

The Message Is:

When students feel cared about, they want to cooperate, not misbehave. Kids know you care when you take the time to find out who they really are, when they feel listened to, and when their thoughts and feelings are taken seriously.

You have to touch the heart before you can reach the mind.

—Carter Bayton

Figure 1.2 Faculty members who make a positive impact on the lives of children.

What Is a Teacher?

A teacher is many things:
She is knowledge with a smile on her face.
He is democracy with a book in his hand.
She is wisdom with a smudge of chalk across her eyebrow.
A teacher has to be an authority on soccer,
grasshoppers, Lear jets, dinosaurs, young love, and music.
—and how to live three months of the year without a
paycheck!

Teachers can be found after school wiping blackboards,
rehearsing plays, coaching football games, correcting papers,
—or just sitting at a desk waiting for the strength to go home!

Unappreciated at times, harried, and overworked,
they will still admit they have the greatest job of all.
And they have!
They are the future of the nation!

BASIC TECHNIQUES OF POSITIVE TEACHERS

When we see truly effective teachers, we are looking at people who are warm and caring. Whether men or women, they are dedicated to being positive and supportive persons who strive to make a difference with children. Much of what they teach is an "invisible curriculum" that is just as important as a concept or skill. Without even thinking, they practice the following basic courtesies with children, which they offer to you:

1. *Smile.* Make it sincere; smile with your eyes too. A smile says, "I'm here to help you. I care."

2. *Say "please." Say "thank you" and "you're welcome."* Model basic courtesy and kindness with these words.

3. *Use a person's name.* Never forget how important a name is to a child.

4. *Listen.* Stop and really hear what the child is saying. Let your face show your interest.

5. *Take time.* You may have very little, but time is so valuable. Remember that, to a child, time translates to love.

I Care About Kids

- I demonstrate that I like them.
- I accept all kids as they are.
- I acknowledge that each child has something to contribute.
- I show my confidence in my students.
- I treat each child without prejudice or partiality.
- I help all children feel they belong.
- I help children accept each other.
- I respect the confidence of a student.
- I uphold promises and agreements with students.
- I avoid making remarks that may discredit others.
- I actively listen when a child speaks.
- I share things about myself.
- I spend time with children who need more of me.
- I admit "I don't know."
- I attempt to understand the unlikable kid.
- I help every student in my class feel successful.

STANDARD PROCEDURES: THE UNWRITTEN RULES

At the basis of a good teacher's philosophy for running her classroom lies a set of procedures that she wants her students to follow. These procedures, or class behaviors, help her maintain a smoothly run classroom, and are known as standard procedures. As a teacher you can create your own personal set of procedures as a guide to cooperation and problem prevention.

Very often you, the teacher, are one of the most stable persons in a child's life, unfortunate but true. It is only if you are lucky that a good percentage of your students come from homes where effective discipline is promoted, where limits are set and rules are consistently followed. More commonly, in the rapidly changing lives of today's families, at all socioeconomic levels, many children have little stability at home. Frequently rules are few, and poor guidelines are provided for children's behavior. Some come to school unprepared to follow rules, to cooperate, or to respect adult authority. Quite often this problem originates in a home where the word "stop" doesn't require them to stop, where "no" means "maybe," and where following rules is optional. Unfortunately, children carry these beliefs to school.

The most effective way to help students from such a wide range of home situations is to establish well-defined standard procedures, and to uphold them consistently. Consistency is, of course, the operative word. As children learn to depend on a constant and stable set of procedures, confusion is reduced. Cooperation evolves, misbehavior decreases, children learn better, and the teacher finds that the year runs more smoothly.

Begin introducing your standard procedures on the very first day of school, if possible, and cover as many of them as your class is ready for on that day. Then adopt the practice of reviewing and reinforcing the procedures every day for the next two or three weeks.

For the most part, standard procedures are unwritten. They are rarely posted on a chart and only occasionally written in a letter to parents. Taught, modeled, and reviewed, they will become implicit and understood by every student, and their importance cannot be overestimated. Standard procedures are guidelines which create both consistency and security for your students. Basically kids feel secure with known procedures, because they know what's expected of them.

Your personalized procedures will form the backbone of your classroom management!

Basic questions concerning everyday classroom living will be answered as students internalize the standard procedures, questions such as

1. What are the procedures for entering the classroom?

2. When is it okay and not okay to talk to neighbors?

3. When is it okay to leave our seats?

4. Where do we put finished papers?

5. What do we do when our work is finished?

6. How do we respond to the "little freeze bell"?

7. What do we do if we need to go to the bathroom?

8. What happens if we don't finish our work on time?

Figure 1.3   These children know precisely what to do with finished papers. It's a standard procedure.

Figure 1.4   This teacher posts a sign to remind students of the first few activities of the day.

The Message Is:

Standard procedures will form the foundation of a smoothly run classroom, even though they are "written" only in the students' heads. If you enforce them consistently in September, you will thank yourself in March!

SUGGESTED STANDARD PROCEDURES

SP 1: Lining Up

Line up outside the classroom door in an orderly manner. Talk quietly with your friends in line, even though you see children from other classes making the wrong choices about behavior.

SP 2: Entering Classroom

Enter our classroom quietly and respectfully. Hang up backpacks and coats. Put homework or notes in the basket. Take your seat quietly.

Practice and reinforce these first two procedures daily for many days. They will accomplish two tasks for you: They set the tone for the day, and, with constant reinforcement, they lay a groundwork of significance for subsequent standard procedures.

Tell your class, "We are responsible for our own conduct. We stand outside quietly, talking with neighbors, and we are proud of our behavior." Tell them that you hope other teachers will look at your class and think, "She's been given the best students in the school." Acknowledge them as they enter the room and sit down at their desks with no teacher reminders.

SP 3: Talking in Classroom

There will be times when you may talk quietly to neighbors at your desks, and times when no talking is allowed.

Display a two-sided sign at the front which can be reversed as needed. The sign should say "No Talk" on the front and "Quiet Talk" on the back.

SP 4: Getting Up From Seats

Please stay seated during class work time; I will explain to you when you may walk around in the classroom and where to get your class materials.

When explaining your standard procedures, keep the lessons simple and concrete. Don't assume that words will be enough, but spend time demonstrating and modeling the correct behavior. When your students forget or get it wrong, practice until they get it right. When the students see you devote so much time and energy to teaching these procedures, they will begin to realize that you are serious about them. "Practice is crucial," warns a veteran teacher. "The beginning of the year is the time to teach and re-teach all important procedures. It usually takes several weeks, but the initial time invested pays huge dividends throughout the year."

SP 5: Pencils Sharpened

Put your worn-down pencil in the can and take a new one whenever you need to.

SP 6: Finished Papers

Unless I tell you differently, put your finished papers in this tray.

SP 7: What to Do When Work Is Finished

Listen carefully as I explain your choices of silent activities. See suggestions later in this chapter and also in Chapter 5.

SP 8: Little Freeze Bell

Stop where you are when the teacher rings the little freeze bell; freeze and listen to a message or special directions.

SP 9: Getting a Drink of Water

Recess is the time for drinks of water; we're sure you can wait till then. This procedure may change later in the year.

SP 10: Going to the Bathroom

Please raise your hand to be excused for the bathroom. I will always say yes. One at a time, of course!

SP 11: Sending Home Student Work

Each Friday you will take home a folder of your work. Your parents will need to sign a form that tells me they have monitored your work.

SP 12: Unfinished Work

The logical consequence for not completing class work or homework is to lose the privilege of Fun Friday Afternoon. You may finish your work then.

SP 13: Fun Friday Afternoon

As a class we will decide on some fun activities for Fun Friday Afternoons. You are eligible to take part if all of your class work and homework have been completed.

> **Teacher Note**
>
> Teachers who have the fewest discipline problems spend much of their first two weeks teaching and reviewing rules and standard procedures.

> **The Message Is:**
>
> Standard procedures, or SPs, are not the same as rules, which are discussed later in this chapter. SPs are simply "how things operate" in order to establish a smoothly run classroom. Teachers should alter the list at their discretion, adding procedures for going to the library, behavior at assemblies, etc. A good deal of teacher time must be allotted, especially in early months, to introduce, teach, model, role play, and review SPs in clever ways. Believe me, it will pay off!

TOGETHER WE MAKE A DIFFERENCE

Wise teachers will wish to elicit parent support for the final three standard procedures, which concern Friday folders, Fun Friday Afternoons, and the consequences for class work not finished. They also need to explain homework procedures. Therefore, the following three-part letter may be useful to deliver this information, and should be sent home as soon as possible.

Never underestimate the potential value of parent support. Good public relations at the beginning of school is important and will reap rewards later. (See Chapter 5 for more ideas on working with parents.)

Letter to Parents

Dear Parents,

Welcome to a new year and a new classroom for your child!
The following are suggestions for you to help him or her become a better learner and to show that you care. Also, please note the Homework Policy and the Friday Folder Procedure that I have included. It is most helpful if you go over these suggestions with your student.

1. Make sure your child gets 8 or 9 hours of sleep each night.

2. Make sure your child has a good attendance record. Children who fall behind in their work become anxious and frustrated.

3. Read to your child and encourage him or her to read to you. Remember, the best way to learn to read is to read!

4. A good policy regarding children and TV is to watch with them and help them evaluate what they're watching in light of your family's values.

5. Please attend our Back-to-School night on _____. I look forward to meeting you.

Parent support is needed and greatly appreciated. When a problem arises in the classroom, I will make every effort to resolve the matter with your child. But if we are unable to resolve the problem, I may need to ask you for assistance and support. Together we can usually resolve problems early and get the child back on track.

_____

Teacher's signature

Copyright © 2005 by Corwin Press. All rights reserved. Reprinted from *Teach More and Discipline Less: Preventing Problem Behaviors in the K–6 Classroom*, by Barbara Reider. Thousand Oaks, CA: Corwin Press, www.corwinpress.com. Reproduction authorized only for the local school site that has purchased this book.

Homework Policy

Homework assignments serve specific purposes. Students need practice with new skills or concepts, and they need to brush up on old ones.

Each week, homework assignments will be sent home with the students in this class on _____ and are due on _____ for full credit.

Parents often have concerns about homework. They wonder how many reminders and how much help they should give. Basically parents must remember that it is the child's responsibility to do the homework. Parents may help in these five ways:

1. Decide with your child on a time that homework will be done each day, building a consistent, regular routine. Insist on absolute quiet during study time.

2. Set up a working place, preferably a desk or table with good light—a place of his own—which delivers the message that studying is valued in this home.

3. Avoid giving more than one reminder that it's time to do homework.

4. Be available for brief help when needed. The message is "I'm here to help, but I won't do the work for you."

5. Explain clearly in advance the logical consequence you will be using when homework is not completed. Examples of consequences are loss of after-school play privileges, no visiting with friends, and no TV or video games.

Copyright © 2005 by Corwin Press. All rights reserved. Reprinted from *Teach More and Discipline Less: Preventing Problem Behaviors in the K–6 Classroom,* by Barbara Reider. Thousand Oaks, CA: Corwin Press, www.corwinpress.com. Reproduction authorized only for the local school site that has purchased this book.

Friday Folder Procedure and Fun Friday Afternoon

Almost all of your child's completed work for the week will be sent home on Friday in his Friday work folder. Please look over the work, offering praise when appropriate. Sign the folder, make any comments you desire, and return the folder with your child on Monday.

Students in this class who have completed all of their assignments, including homework, by Friday noon are eligible for participation in Fun Friday Afternoon, a preferred activity time.

Students who are not eligible will use that time to catch up on remaining work. Any work not completed on Friday afternoon will be noted in the folder and sent home to be done over the weekend and returned for partial credit on Monday.

Copyright © 2005 by Corwin Press. All rights reserved. Reprinted from *Teach More and Discipline Less: Preventing Problem Behaviors in the K–6 Classroom*, by Barbara Reider. Thousand Oaks, CA: Corwin Press, www.corwinpress.com. Reproduction authorized only for the local school site that has purchased this book.

THE POWER OF A QUIET VOICE

A teacher in San Francisco, who is also an author, titled one of her books *Good Morning, Class. I Love You.* I know that my friend Esther Wright doesn't actually say these very words each morning. She doesn't have to. She lives them; she constantly demonstrates them.

One of Mrs. Wright's techniques is to speak, invariably, in a calm, quiet tone of voice. She suggests that we teachers listen to ourselves as we speak to students, since some of us may be completely unaware of our tone of voice and volume. We can remember to speak in low, well-modulated, courteous voices, demonstrating to students that we respect them and want them to speak quietly also.

Teachers who have trained themselves to speak in a lower tone of voice tell of amazing changes in their classrooms. Some of their comments are

The children listen better and now they're also lowering their voices.

My whole class calms down when they have to concentrate. They like it, and it makes my room much more pleasant.

Teacher Note

Never speak when someone is talking. *Never* try to talk over the noise. Stop. Ring a quiet bell, if needed. Wait. Begin *only* when you have students' attention.

The Message Is:

At all times of your day, keep a quiet, calm demeanor. Let your voice remain uniformly low. Try playing a little classical music softly in the background. Turn on a soft lamp. These things are very calming to the children.

MINIMIZE PROBLEMS AS YOU ARRANGE DESKS

Effective teachers carefully arrange the desks in their classrooms on the first day of school and just as carefully assign students to designated seats. These first arrangements will probably be temporary, but their goals are valid. Teachers wish to maximize learning, implement classroom management, and minimize behavior problems. These teachers declare that it is important to observe two basic procedures regarding desk arrangements and assignments:

1. Desk arrangements must allow the teacher to move around the room quickly and easily. Many arrangements meet this criterion, but one good suggestion is the "capital E" arrangement, where desks are placed in two letter E's facing each other. (See diagram.) In this way all students can see the front board, and the teacher can walk within the center to supervise each student.

2. Carefully assigned seats should be calculated to prevent problems. Two types of students will be seated near the front of the room: those who may need help with class work, and those who are potential disrupters. Independent workers and those capable of working together may be seated at the sides, the back rows, and the corners of the E.

Do not hesitate to make frequent changes in seating as the weeks progress. As the class works and interacts, observe behavior and interpersonal relations. Take notes, and when the class leaves for the day, make desk changes accordingly. Experienced teachers claim that classroom management is greatly improved simply by wise placement of students' desks.

Teacher Note

You will have a more effective class from the first if you assign students to their desks. However, as a feeling of trust and cooperation builds within your group, students may be allowed to request desk changes. Wise teachers require a good behavior agreement between the parties involved.

Figure 1.5 "Capital E" desk arrangement.

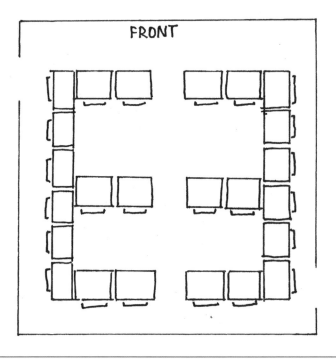

Figure 1.6 Diagram of "Capital E" desk arrangement.

Figure 1.7 In a smoothly run classroom, students know what to do when work is done.

The Message Is:

Make the effort to structure the physical environment and you will reduce the occurrence of problems.

"TEACHER, WHAT DO I DO NOW?"

Students need to know what to do when their work is done. This standard procedure (number 7 on our list) is very important in terms of a smooth-running classroom. In fact, your entire management plan can fall apart during these transition times if children who finish their work either interrupt you for directions or begin playing around.

There are many options from which you, the teacher, can choose. The most simple is to post a list of choices. One clever teacher has devised a small chart with cards that fit into three slots. The chart is headed, "THREE SILENT CHOICES." Written on the cards are three of the following suggestions, to be changed frequently:

- Magazine Rack
- Pillows 'N' Books
- Art Cart
- Activity Workbooks
- Puzzle Place
- Science Table
- Quick Draw Station
- Clay Corner

Obviously, a small bit of teacher set-up time is required for the three choices, the simpler the better being the key.

Some teachers suggest a "Free-Time Writing Activity" for students who have finished their work early. Each week a quick and easy writing idea is displayed on a card and accompanied by a small pile of paper.

Free-Time Writing Activities

- List five jobs you'd enjoy doing in your lifetime.
- You are in a jungle. Describe what you see, hear, and touch.
- List 13 lucky things that have happened in your life.
- Write 20 things that you wonder about.
- Write a surprise welcome-home note to your mom or dad.
- Tell what makes you grouchy. What makes your mom grouchy?
- Pick an unusual word in the dictionary. Write two definitions, one real and one fake. Can someone guess which is fake?
- Write a sentence using each word in alphabetical order. "Annie bites carrots diligently . . ."
- List 10 essential items you'd take on a camping trip.
- Create 10 exciting new holidays to add to the year's calendar.
- Name five of your all-time favorite characters from books.
- If you had no paper, no telephone, no computer, how would you send a message to a friend in another town?
- List and illustrate 10 things that are green.
- Delicious. Parallelogram. Biplane. List your 20 favorite words.
- Write a thank-you note to tell your teacher of 10 things you like about this school year.
- Describe the most beautiful place you've ever visited.
- List 10 things that make you smile, your teacher smile, and your mom or dad smile.
- List five questions you would like to ask the principal.
- List five things you would like to tell your teacher.

CLASSROOM RULES ARE SET COOPERATIVELY

In addition to standard procedures, you will need to establish a few general rules of classroom conduct. Rules are needed in every classroom, and they should be set up cooperatively by you and your students. To do this you will need to conduct a meaningful discussion with your class, whether it be first or eighth grade. This discussion is actually an invitation for students to describe the class they would like to be part of and to make their suggestions for class rules. It is helpful to conduct this discussion on one of the very first days of school.

Discussion Questions About Rules

1. What makes a good classroom?
2. What is a good teacher like?
3. What are good students like?
4. What kinds of behaviors can ruin a class?
5. What rules might be helpful in our class?
6. What should happen if a child breaks a rule?
7. Who can suggest a good rule for our list?

The importance of the discussion is the discussion itself, just as meaningful, in fact, as the list of rules that will result. There is untold value in encouraging students to think about and decide upon the behaviors and work habits they believe are important. You, of course, will steer the discussion toward the points you want covered, and you will ensure that they include

- Careful listening
- Doing their best work
- Being responsible for their own learning
- Respect and kindness toward others

When the list of rules is decided upon, compliment your class on their cooperation. "This is our learning environment, and together we are responsible for making it work!" Have a student copy the rules onto a permanent chart to be posted in the room. Also, when each student makes a copy, send them home with reminders that "in our class, everybody makes the rules."

> **Teacher Note**
>
> Students know that you respect and care about them when they are consulted and involved in decision making. Teachers who fear a loss of control will find that when student input is encouraged, control is seldom needed.

The Message Is:

Students who have "ownership" in setting up rules are much more likely to follow them.

Figure 1.8   Rules chosen by student consensus.

Figure 1.9   Rules posted by a teacher.

REMINDERS ABOUT RULES

1. There should be relatively few classroom rules (five or less).

2. Rules should be set up cooperatively.

3. Parents need to be aware of class rules.

4. Reinforce students who are following the rules.

5. Remind students, "These are *our* rules; we made them together."

6. Rules must be enforced every time they are broken. Failure to finish work, for example, requires a child to make up the work at recess time. (See Chapter 6 for more help with the use of logical consequences.)

7. Students like rules and appreciate a well-managed classroom.

8. If a rule isn't working, discuss and change it.

> **Teacher Note**
>
> Let your students know that rules show how you expect them to behave in the classroom. Motivate them to follow the rules because it is the right thing to do, and it leads to a better classroom for everyone.

> **The Message Is:**
>
> You, the teacher, must be consistent about sticking to the rules. Be the same every day. If your behavior varies, children will never stop testing you! Show them that you say what you mean and mean what you say.

RECOGNITION AND REINFORCEMENT

You can set yourself up for success by reinforcing good behavior on the very first week of school. Let's look again at SP 7 (What to do when work is finished) as an example of how easy it can be. Posted in your classroom is a list of activities from which students may choose when their work is finished, such as a Three Silent Choices list.

Here is the set-up: Your students are working on an assignment at their desks. Wait until one child finishes his work. Notice as he puts his paper on the tray for finished work, stops to briefly read over the list of choices, makes his decision, and perhaps chooses a fun reading book.

At that precise moment, say aloud to the class, "I've noticed that when one of you was finished, he checked our list and chose the activity he preferred. Nice going."

It is this kind of reinforcement technique which must be used with each of your SPs as it comes up, until all students have demonstrated that they know each and every standard procedure and it has become a habit or routine!

The importance of the first day and first week cannot be over-emphasized. In any good book about classroom management, you can read these words over and over: "Establish your rules and procedures carefully and you will reap the benefits all year." The actual first day and week will become almost boring with all of the redundant but crucial practice and review.

> ### The Message Is:
>
> Consistency is the key—until each rule and procedure is very clear, and there is no doubt in anyone's mind about how to behave in this classroom. Each successful incidence must be recognized and reinforced. You truly are setting yourself up for success!

Unfortunately, a sound emphasis on standard procedures and class rules is occasionally treated lightly by teachers who overlook their importance at the beginning of the year. Educator/author Fred Jones warns, "A cavalier approach to rules will stress not only the class management system but also the teacher's body throughout the school year, a brutal price to pay for having shortchanged a crucial topic."

As teachers we have a choice. Either we begin early, take the time to teach and reinforce the rules, or we exhaust ourselves trying to mend fences later in the year.

ROUNDUP OF CHAPTER 1

1. Begin teaching outside the classroom door.

2. Engender respect by your presence and demeanor.

3. Strive to develop strategies of good classroom management.

4. With your first words, deliver a message of caring.

5. Start immediately to teach your standard procedures.

6. Practice and review SPs for complete understanding.

7. Never underestimate the importance of SPs.

8. Inform parents of the homework policy and Friday procedures, and elicit their support.

9. Carefully calculate your seating arrangement.

10. Arrange your student desks to allow for quick, easy teacher movement.

11. Purposefully build a habit within yourself of speaking with a calm, quiet tone of voice.

12. Let your students take part in setting rules.

13. Enforce the rules as well as the SPs with unwavering consistency.

2 Build Rapport With Kids

THE SECRETS TO THEIR SUCCESS

How is it that some teachers are immediately able to establish a feeling of rapport with their students, without fail, every single year? Why does it look so effortless? What do they know that we don't know?

When I have invited the "old pro" teachers—those who obviously have mastered their craft—to reveal the secrets of their success, the irony is that they can't readily explain them. "I don't have problems with misbehavior," they say, "but I don't exactly know why."

To these master teachers, discipline just isn't an issue, but when encouraged they do divulge some common practices. They say

I start by really getting to know the students.

I try to set up a special one-to-one relationship with each child as soon as possible.

I begin immediately to establish trust.

You have to build a sense of rapport with kids right from the first.

I realize that what I do on the first days of school greatly influences whether I win or lose my class for the year.

I start by trying immediately to figure out what makes each one tick . . . especially those who are trying to show off or push my buttons.

COMMON DENOMINATORS

Among the comments collected from these exemplary teachers, there seem to be two common denominators. The first is that these teachers *consciously begin to build rapport* the minute they meet their students. Convinced that first impressions count, and recognizing that shyness is a feeling within many children, they meet their classes each day with "welcome" written all over their faces.

The second common denominator is that these teachers *try to really get to know their students.* They realize the importance of accepting and appreciating each individual personality.

"Who are these children in my classroom?" they seem to be asking. "What are their interests? Which of them is shy or outgoing? What are their family backgrounds? How many have shaky self-esteem? How many are covering low self-esteem with misbehavior? What are their strengths and weaknesses? Which ones will need my special attention?"

Children come to school in different shapes and sizes, personality types and learning styles, backgrounds and capabilities. All want and need to be heard, accepted, and understood. All want and need to succeed in the classroom, socially and academically. All want and need to feel liked and valued.

In this chapter we will examine the methods and techniques of teachers who possess the uncanny ability to build rapport with every child, even the most difficult.

Teachers will be described in this chapter as "classroom counselors" whose job it is to know and understand each individual child. Beginning teachers as well as veterans will find themselves with this additional title, and hopefully will welcome it. For only with understanding can teachers build the necessary rapport, plan instruction, and meet the needs of everyone. As counselors, teachers must look behind the behavior, discover the feelings driving that which is self-defeating, and learn to meet the problems that result.

TWO LETTERS OF WELCOME

Recognizing the value of a head start, some begin the task even before school starts, by means of a welcoming letter in the mail. For example, this letter goes to each of Mrs. Burke's first graders one week before school starts. Very short, and printed in words a first grader might be able to read, it says,

> I'm glad that you will be in my class this year. We will learn many new things and have fun. Please come to Room 4. I will see you next Monday.
>
> Love, Mrs. Burke

However, the welcoming letter from Mr. Douglas to his fifth graders is two pages long. He introduces himself and tells of his interests. His letter begins, "The good news is that you'll be in my class this year! I want to get to know you, what you are like, and what you're interested in. And I'll tell you about myself, too. I know how to fly an airplane and I like to teach students about flight. Also, I'm a big 49ers and Kings fan."

Mr. Douglas lists the major projects that his class will be doing, carefully explains the behavior expectations, and shares the "secrets for student success" in his classroom, including respect and responsibility. By writing this letter, he strives to be known to his students as a person, not just a teacher, and to begin the trust-building process.

Some teachers wait until the end of the first week of school to send an "off to a fine start" note. The long-term results of these initial letters home are often very significant. The communication with parents establishes a cooperative relationship when they realize the teacher is truly interested in their child. This bond can be particularly important in cases where students are likely to receive negative feedback at some time later in the year. Good public relations at the beginning of the year helps to guarantee parent support.

First-Week Note Home to Students

Dear _____ ,

We are off to a good start this first week. Everything is new and different, and sometimes new things are hard to get used to, but I notice that all of you are trying to learn "the ropes."

First, you are all very friendly to each other, and especially to the new students in school. You're making friends, and this will help us create a better classroom atmosphere.

Second, you're picking up on our procedures, like lining up and coming into the classroom. You remember to raise your hands to participate, and you're careful to work quietly. And you did an excellent job creating our class rules, which I'm sure you shared at home.

I think this will be a wonderful year and we'll learn a lot. I'm proud of you!

See you next week,

_____

Teacher's signature

Copyright © 2005 by Corwin Press. All rights reserved. Reprinted from *Teach More and Discipline Less: Preventing Problem Behaviors in the K–6 Classroom* by Barbara Reider. Thousand Oaks, CA: Corwin Press, www.corwinpress.com. Reproduction authorized only for the local school site that has purchased this book.

The Message Is:

A wise teacher knows that it is not only *children* who read letters which arrive home at the first of the school year, but also *parents*. You can, through a welcome letter, or a note the first week, begin to build the "three-way partnership" (teacher-student-parent) that is necessary for school success.

GETTING TO KNOW YOU

One of our first jobs as caring teachers is to get to know our students better. In any average classroom we will find ourselves dealing with a wide range of abilities, maturity levels, readiness, and motivation. Self-esteem levels will differ, as will personalities, interests, and feelings. Some of these characteristics can be discovered with a student inventory, which kids love to fill out either at home or at school. In some classrooms, teachers facilitate an "interview circle" to help everyone get to know each other.

Student Inventory

1. My name is _____ and I was born in _____

   _____ .

2. The one thing I like best about my family is _____

   _____ .

3. I really like my home because _____

   _____ .

4. One word that really describes me is _____ because

   _____ .

5. I love to read about _____

   _____ .

6. When I grow up I'd like to be a _____ because

   _____ .

7. If I had just one wish it would be _____

   _____ .

8. My favorite sport is _____

   _____ .

9. What I like best about myself is _____

   _____ .

10. My best friend is _____ because _____

    _____ .

11. One question I'd like to ask my teacher is_____

    _____ .

Copyright © 2005 by Corwin Press. All rights reserved. Reprinted from *Teach More and Discipline Less: Preventing Problem Behaviors in the K–6 Classroom* by Barbara Reider. Thousand Oaks, CA: Corwin Press, www.corwinpress.com. Reproduction authorized only for the local school site that has purchased this book.

Interview Circle

An interview circle provides another excellent opportunity for students to share their interests and beliefs. For this activity, all participants sit in a large circle, in the middle of which sits the teacher, who has volunteered to model the activity for the class.

The students are permitted to ask you, their teacher, a total of three questions, and you have the right to pass on any question you choose not to answer. The questions may be about sports, hobbies, family, friends, etc.

After three questions a new interviewee is chosen to sit in the circle, this time a student. At the conclusion of the activity, ask the students how they felt about sitting in the interview circle, and how it helped them to know their class members better.

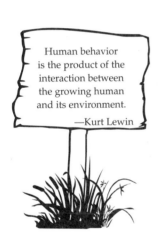

Human behavior is the product of the interaction between the growing human and its environment.

—Kurt Lewin

Figure 2.1   An "interview circle."

THE NEWS BEGINS THE DAY

Your students are settled in their seats at the beginning of the day. Seated on a stool in the front of the room, you smile at each one and enjoy their responses: easy smiles, very shy smiles, or reluctant grins. The message you send is, "We're a good group. Though some of our work will be hard, I believe in you, and if you work hard we'll be successful." The message they send is, "We trust you and we'll do our best because we know you'll help."

Grab this moment! It's your first chance to build the rapport and cohesiveness you need to influence learning!

This is News and Sharing time, which you will begin by sharing something of yourself, a small event of your morning or something you did on the weekend. Be willing to admit doubts and hopes; be sincere with them.

Next ask, "What's happening with you today?" (Or, as I like to say in Spanish, "*Que pasa, clase?*") Encourage your students to share anything that's on their minds and to respond to each other. Be sure to model compassion or delight, building cohesiveness all the while.

AN IMPORTANT 15 MINUTES

In the fifth grade, Mr. Bush, who realizes the value of setting a positive tone for the day, always makes time at the beginning of the day for News and Sharing. One 10-year-old vividly describes yesterday's soccer game, whereupon everybody wants to talk about soccer. A little girl waves her hand and, with shaky voice, reports that her bike was stolen last night. When Mr. Bush recognizes her plea for help and asks for suggestions from the class, the children decide to make signs for their neighborhood. "Call the police," they say. "Call the newspaper." Everyone is upset and eager to help.

Another child announces a new baby on the way in his family, causing someone to wonder aloud just exactly how doctors find out if it's a boy or a girl. Others offer their "expert" opinion on the subject. Now a student shares a "serious problem" about her sister whom the family feels is too young to be pregnant. The class nods sympathetically.

Doug Bush responds to each child with appropriate interest and empathy. He moderates the discussions which unfold, meanwhile scanning the class for potential problems and concerns. He is very cognizant that trust and rapport are being established during this activity. The children are getting to know and respect him and each other as vital individuals, and they are giving and receiving the undivided attention that so many children need. This teacher considers that the time spent in News and Sharing is one of the most important 15 minutes of the day. "This way," says Doug, "I make personal contact with each of my kids."

> **Teacher Note**
>
> At News and Sharing time, do not busy yourself with small tasks such as taking roll or reading notes. Do not have a student preside over this opportunity for building teacher/class rapport. Look at each speaker as he or she contributes; model respectful listening and insist upon it in your students.

Figure 2.2   News and Sharing: "What's happening in your life today?"

The Message Is:

For some children, school is their only safe haven. They may have spent the first two hours of their day in a tragically unhappy home situation. You, the teacher, are saying in effect, "You are safe here. You can count on me and your classmates because we care about you."

CAN YOU RISK SHARING YOURSELF?

"Why should they trust me?" asks Ms. Gulas. "They're 11- and 12-year-olds, and they're beginning to distrust every adult." This sixth-grade teacher, who believes that "rapport is the door to reach the kid," begins to build trust on the first day of school. She shares herself, honestly and sincerely—not only her likes and dislikes but more personally, her hurt feelings when she was ridiculed for trying out for a basketball team. By being this vulnerable, Corinne Gulas, a very well-loved teacher, invites her students to trust her enough to risk sharing themselves.

Taking risks is something she encourages by reading to her students about the lives of famous people who were successful even though others laughed at them. Benjamin Franklin. Thomas Edison. We can think of many more. "There will be people who laugh at you when you succeed and when you fail," she tells students, "but you can risk doing what you think is right, as long as you believe in yourself."

To be a *person* in front of kids is to be vulnerable, and vulnerability is not an easy posture for adults. In his book, *Beyond Discipline,* Alfie Kohn explains that "to reach out to children and develop genuine, warm relationships with them may compromise one's ability to control them. Much of what is wrong with our schools can be traced back to the fact that when these two objectives clash, connection frequently gives way to control."

Ms. Gulas believes that if she can't connect with a child, she won't be able to influence his desire to learn. And obviously her connections are long-lasting, for many former students come back to visit her every year.

A positive classroom climate enhances motivation and improves behavior.

Figure 2.3   An atmosphere of trust is built by caring teachers.

CLASSROOM CLIMATE

In the preface of this book, classroom climate was defined as the atmosphere or the "feeling in the air" within a classroom. This feeling is an energy that either contributes to or detracts from a child's social development and opportunity to learn. And who is in charge of creating the climate? Of course it is the classroom teacher! Anyone who has read the classic how-to-teach book *Teacher and Child* will recall the oft-quoted preface written by author Haim Ginott when he was a young teacher:

> I have come to a frightening conclusion. I am the decisive element in my classroom. It is my personal approach that creates the

climate. It is my daily mood that makes the weather. As a teacher I possess tremendous power to make a child's life miserable or joyous. I can be a tool of torture or an instrument of inspiration. I can humiliate or humor, hurt or heal. In all situations it is my response that decides whether a crisis will be escalated or de-escalated, and a child humanized or de-humanized.

Indeed the responsibility and the privilege of creating a positive environment falls on the shoulders of every teacher. According to Jeanne Gibbs, author of *Tribes,* a positive class climate evolves from a teacher-created atmosphere of trust.

You may have had the opportunity to step into a classroom with just such a positive climate. You may have noticed a feeling of warmth and acceptance which is inviting and involving. This is an affirming place, where no put-downs are allowed and where it is safe to make mistakes and even to fail. Here the classroom management is orchestrated with skill and care.

Techniques that help the teacher build a caring classroom climate are found throughout this book, but one stands alone in its simplicity and impact: Establish a special one-to-one relationship with each and every child. With some children this takes one week; with others, insecure or wary or unable to trust, it may take two months. Use every method you can think of to establish these significant relationships, including small personal conversations, private winks, or unseen pats on the back. Attempt to know each one better.

The payoff for building a positive climate is children who feel better about themselves and others, and who have a high sense of self-esteem. "High self-esteem not only correlates to positive behavior," declares Gibbs, "but to greater academic achievement."

YES, YOU ARE A COUNSELOR

If you are a beginning teacher, you may find yourself wearing many different hats. You may wear the hat of a coach, a psychologist, a nurse, a disciplinarian, a friend, or perhaps the hat of a part-time parent. It's all a part of the job. One hat that you will wear with special pride is the hat of a counselor, for effective teachers infuse their teaching with counseling. What jobs will you perform in your counselor hat?

- You will listen and try to understand.
- You will befriend and encourage.
- You will accept and care.
- You will diagnose and try to remediate problems.

And you will walk around part of the time with a perplexed look on your face, as if to say, "What is it with that kid? Why is he acting this way? What's driving his behavior? What can I do to help him?"

Teachers eventually realize that the hardest problems to solve are those that involve low self-esteem. They notice a child misbehaving . . . acting like a class clown or a showoff, a bully, a persistent interrupter, or a fight-instigator. All of these misbehaviors point to a lack of self-esteem. According to educator Harry Wong, "Lack of self-esteem is the major reason that students act up."

Teachers also notice children exhibiting self-defeating behavior: a child who is a follower, a painfully shy child who can't risk taking part, a child who is a whiner and a blamer, or a completely irresponsible child. These are also behaviors that point to a lack of self-esteem.

Children with low self-esteem who exhibit either misbehavior or self-defeating behavior do so as a result of certain underlying feelings: feelings of inadequacy; feelings of powerlessness; feelings of isolation and loneliness. These are the feelings driving the behavior which you, the teacher-counselor, will be challenged to diagnose and remedy.

The Message Is:

Children who misbehave in class are a real challenge to your classroom management! Much of this self-defeating behavior is a result of low self-esteem, which is not always recognized by other adults. The courageous teacher will meet the challenge, realizing that it is not just our job, but our opportunity and privilege!

Teacher Note

Remember that, to a child, time translates to love. Anything you can do to make children feel good about themselves will help to minimize discipline problems.

The hardest children to love are those who need it the most.

THE CHARACTERISTICS OF HIGH SELF-ESTEEM

In order to help children with self-esteem issues, it is beneficial to recognize those with high, solid self-esteem, and to be aware of the characteristics that we can help other children achieve.

Children With High Self-Esteem
Work Cooperatively With Others

These children consistently check with others in their small group to make sure they're all on the right track. They show respect and consideration for others' opinions. They find fair ways to take turns or solve problems. They don't have a need to be first, or sit in front, or always be right.

Children With High Self-Esteem
Usually Have a Wide Circle of Friends

These children play fair, try hard to cooperate, and find ways to let everyone play the game. They express warmth and caring and concern for others; camaraderie comes easily.

Children With High Self-Esteem Often Set
High Standards for Themselves; They Work Toward Goals

These kids attempt projects which others wouldn't touch, ready to try though risking failure. They determine to reach difficult goals, such as reading 60 books, or building a model of a molecule. They seem to have a sense of direction toward which they strive, whether it be short-term, such as learning times tables, or long-term, such as pitching for the Major Leagues.

Children With High Self-Esteem Take Pride in Their
Accomplishments, But Need Little Outside Recognition

These children feel intrinsic pride and require minimal praise from teachers, parents, or friends. They may write wonderfully imaginative stories, or play the piano with magic fingers; they seem quietly happy with their accomplishments and need few extrinsic rewards.

Children With High Self-Esteem
Take Responsibility for Their Actions

When these children make mistakes, they do not blame others, or make excuses, or whine about the error. Rather, they realize that it's okay to make a mistake, and better to try to learn from it. They have faith in "next time."

Children With High Self-Esteem Are Generally Aware of Their Own Strengths and Weaknesses

These children are the kind who will admit, "I'm not too good in basketball, but I'm making improvements." They willingly ask for help in the area that is difficult for them, and take pride in their stronger areas.

Children With High Self-Esteem Are Not Afraid to Express Their Opinions

These children do their own thinking and assertively express *their* ideas or suggestions, even those which may be unconventional or unpopular. Moreover, they readily award this inalienable right to others as well.

Children With High Self-Esteem Generally Have an Optimistic View of Life

These kids maintain confidence in their capabilities, seem to genuinely like their schoolmates, and remain optimistic through the day's ups and downs. They are not threatened by failure but look forward to doing a better job next time.

THREE COMPONENTS OF SELF-ESTEEM

Veteran teachers have watched these children with high self-esteem walk into their classrooms on the first day of every school year. They recognize that these kids "just feel good about themselves." They are ready to make new friends, ready to like and be liked by others. Happy and confident, they are pretty sure they'll be able to do the work.

It is now an established fact that a child's success in school can be predicted by determining how he feels about himself at an early age. Once we believed that I.Q. was the major criterion—and undeniably it is important—but research now tells us that the correlation between self-esteem and school achievement is as high as between I.Q. and school achievement. It is little wonder that good teachers look closely at their students' behavior—behavior that reveals their self-esteem.

When you notice habitual misbehavior or self-defeating behavior, train yourself to closely consider the three components of self-esteem. These three are a sense of connectedness, a sense of uniqueness, and a sense of power. Use these components to pinpoint a child's needs in order to help him build self-esteem.

BUILDING A SENSE OF CONNECTEDNESS

Some children feel very comfortable in a group. They join clubs or teams, or organize their own clubs. They communicate and relate easily with others; they feel wanted and liked. These children have a high sense of connectedness.

On the other hand, some children feel uncomfortable in almost any group, so they spend a lot of time alone. They badly need friends but lack the skills to make friends. They feel lonely in their isolation. These children have a low sense of connectedness.

As you recognize the behavior and the feelings of such children, you may use the following suggestions to help them raise their self-esteem by building a sense of connectedness:

1. Let this child know you care about him, with a special wink, a thumbs-up, and a pat as you go by. Find a little time to give him your undivided attention.

2. Find situations when this child can work with a partner, studying spelling, making a map, taking measurements, etc.

3. Reinforce cooperative work when you see it. "You worked well with Eric today." When you see him playing with another child outside, tell him about it.

The Message Is:

Teachers like to connect with people, and we like kids with a high sense of connectedness. Although we often become frustrated with those who hang on us, hoping for attention, we can learn just how to help these loners.

Catch this kid connecting with others!

Figure 2.4   Sometimes you don't feel comfortable in a group.

A human being's strongest motivation is to belong.

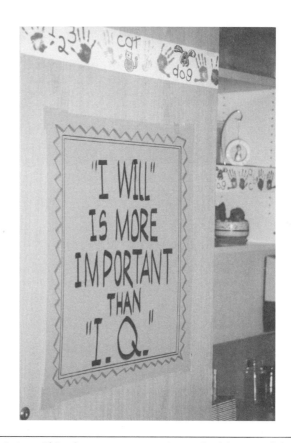

Figure 2.5   This classroom motto aims at building confident kids.

A Sense of Connectedness

High Sense of Connectedness

This child

- Feels he belongs
- Feels he is part of the class, group, or team
- Communicates and relates to others
- Is sensitive and empathic to others
- Feels important, noticed, wanted, and liked
- Is often happily nonchalant
- Is easy to like and often envied by others

Low Sense of Connectedness

This child

- Rarely raises his hand to participate
- Doesn't know how to relate; communicates reluctantly
- Spends much time alone
- Keeps hurts to himself
- May retreat to favorite toys, etc. for comfort
- Is always on your heels

Friendships, however, are terribly important.

How to Build a Sense of Connectedness

- Simply say, "Hi," and smile or wink.
- Show affection physically with a pat or hug.
- Model sharing yourself and your feelings.
- Listen without judging and avoid questioning.
- Provide opportunities for group work or play.
- Ignore acting out for attention.
- Give attention for appropriate behavior.
- Praise instances of successful relationships.

BUILDING A SENSE OF UNIQUENESS

Many children have been encouraged at home to do their own thinking, to use their imaginations, and to be creative. They are the students who express their own opinions. Teachers notice that they're full of ideas. These children have a high sense of uniqueness.

But some children are convinced they aren't worthy or special in any way. Some will conform to the opinions of others. We call them followers; they lack self-confidence. Some are misbehavers, seeking the attention they need by showing off or making smart remarks.

A child with a low sense of uniqueness can be helped if teachers remember that by choosing this inappropriate behavior the child is crying out for attention and recognition, two basic needs in all of us.

Three suggestions to build a sense of uniqueness are

1. Find something that this child does that is appropriate, and build on it. Maybe he's nice to little kids, good at drawing, an expert on hot air balloons, or clever at jokes. Give him recognition, which he so sorely needs.

2. Lead discussion about *me* to help this child find his special qualities. Someday I'd like to. . . . It's easy for me to. . . . In my free time I. . . .

3. Praise him in private and reprimand him in private.

The Message Is:

It is highly likely that nobody at home is giving this child the attention and recognition he needs, so out of discouragement he has chosen to misbehave in order to get it. Teachers can do wonders to help if we bear in mind, "There is no such thing as a bad child, only discouraged."

Teacher Note

Kids are basically sweet; they are all born that way. And a child who is misbehaving, for one reason or another, is saying inside, "I wish someone would just recognize there are some things I can do. Why doesn't anyone notice?"

Catch this kid doing something good!

A Sense of Uniqueness

High Sense of Uniqueness

This child

- Knows he is somebody special
- Feels he can do things no one else can do
- Trusts himself and his perceptions
- Expresses himself in his own special style
- Uses imagination and creativity
- Is liked by teachers for his cleverness and uniqueness, even when showing off

Low Sense of Uniqueness

This child

- Is convinced that he is just not special
- May be a conformist and a follower
- Mimics others and is rarely creative or imaginative
- May be a chronic behavior problem
- Seeks recognition by showing off inappropriately
- Will prove a specialness even though it is negative

How to Build a Sense of Uniqueness

- Help child identify his special qualities.
- Give many opportunities for success: artistic, physical, academic, or verbal.
- Especially promote and encourage creativity, use of imagination, and individuality.
- Jot little notes to this child, and give private praise.
- Constantly communicate acceptance.

BUILDING A SENSE OF POWER

A child with a high sense of power is a risk-taker who believes he can do what he sets out to do. He feels that, to a reasonable extent, he is in charge of his life; he can look at his options and make his own decisions. He welcomes responsibility and enjoys solving problems.

Teacher Note

Take a new, creative approach to problems.

Look at self-defeating behavior with a much wiser eye.

Ask yourself, "How must this child be feeling?"

But some children shirk responsibility and will use any excuse to get out of work. They may be whiners who blame all bad results on someone else. They may manipulate others to do their work. Children with a low sense of power are very frustrating to the teacher.

A low sense of power, like all self-esteem, begins at home, but it, too, can be remedied. Three suggestions for building a sense of power are

1. Begin by conferring with this child's parents, especially if you feel they are overprotective. Describe what is ahead for their child if he continues to shirk responsibility.

2. Hold the child responsible for all schoolwork. Refuse to listen to excuses from whiners, but praise any diligent work and wise decisions.

3. Provide opportunities for decision making by offering choices and alternatives in his schoolwork. Give approval for good choices in friends and work.

Catch this kid taking responsibility!

Figure 2.6   Being responsible for assignments starts young.

Figure 2.7   Fourth graders make choices of learning modes.

A Sense of Power

High Sense of Power

This child

- Feels he is in control of his life
- Checks his options and alternatives
- Believes he can do what he sets out to do
- Makes decisions, solves problems, meets challenges, and takes risks
- Deals with pressure and stress successfully
- Seeks opportunities to excel

Low Sense of Power

This child

- Feels he has little influence over his life
- Likely has failed academically and has poor skills
- Is afraid of failing again, and gives up easily

(Continued)

(Continued)

- Avoids risks, challenges, and all problems
- Avoids taking responsibility; inveigles others into doing his work, including parents and teachers
- Is a whiner and a blamer, and is often called "spoiled"

How to Build a Sense of Power

- Diagnose and reteach needed skills.
- Constantly provide small opportunities for decision making by offering choices and alternatives.
- Start with small problems to be solved.
- Build confidence by ensuring success whenever possible.
- Give approval for independent choices in work and play.

ROUNDUP OF CHAPTER 2

1. Remember that effective teachers begin immediately to build rapport.

2. Good teachers truly care for their students.

3. Send a welcome letter before school starts.

4. Smile. Say "please" and "thank you." Use students' names. Listen. Take time.

5. Conduct an interview circle to get to know everyone.

6. News and Sharing time is an excellent opportunity for building rapport.

7. Build trust by sharing your own feelings.

8. Recognize that a caring class climate is a foundation block of classroom management, and it is *you* who creates that climate!

9. Look carefully at the self-esteem of your students, especially the misbehavers.

10. Give a little special time to a child with a low sense of connectedness.

11. Find something good about a child with a low sense of uniqueness.

12. Recognize a low sense of power and catch this child being responsible.

3 Develop Effective Strategies

LOVE ALONE DOES NOT A CLASSROOM MANAGE

"It is the undying hope of young teachers that if they just love children hard enough and try hard enough, everything will turn out just fine," says Fred Jones in *Positive Classroom Discipline.*

But every experienced teacher knows that love is not enough. Neither is creating rapport nor establishing trust. "Friendly attitudes do not classroom problems solve," Haim Ginott reminds us in *Teacher and Child.* And he is right. A teacher can be warm, patient, and loving and still be unable to survive in today's classroom.

Effective, workable strategies are required. Good teaching occurs when skillful, caring professionals adapt these strategies to specific situations and students, using professional judgment to decide what approach works for each situation.

Demonstrating how this powerful combination of caring and skill is put into practice is one of the purposes of Chapter 3. Described on these pages are masterful, sometimes ingenious methods used by a diversity of teachers at all grade levels. Their efforts are directed toward building a classroom climate with optimum opportunities for learning.

PLANNING: THE KEY TO GOOD TEACHING

"I never leave my classroom at the end of the day," says master teacher Arlene Barooshian, "until my plans for the next day are made, and all materials are ready." This teacher is preparing for tomorrow, not for a substitute but for herself, acting on her belief that good teaching requires careful planning.

Many years of practice have brought Mrs. B. to this viewpoint. Using her professional experience, she matches strategies, activities, and materials with her students' abilities, always taking into consideration developmental levels as well as learning styles. She provides for those in her class who are struggling to learn as well as those who zip through every new concept. "To make things run smoothly tomorrow, I stay here tonight," she declares. "You ask about classroom management . . . I avoid confusion, misbehavior, and wasted time by having things ready in advance."

Effective teachers invest time and effort into the prevention of discipline problems in one major way: by planning well-organized interesting lessons. As we watch Mrs. Barooshian teach Reading to her students, we see that she first presents a lesson to the entire class, then divides the students into small groups to begin their work. We notice that the teacher sits with each small group at a side reading table, while others work at their desks.

Today's lesson, on changing word endings, has been subdivided into several related assignments according to the capabilities of each group. One assignment, requiring students to use both past and present parts of speech, is calculated for an advanced group of busy story-writers. Other assignments are geared for a second and third group.

In this manner, each student has an assignment pertaining to the main lesson of the day and prepared for his individual needs. Obviously, all assignments were crafted long before the students arrived at school.

Mrs. Barooshian knows that, as their Reading teacher, she must (1) gain a solid understanding of each child's developmental level and capability, (2) place the children accordingly into groups, and (3) plan each group's assignments. Meeting the diverse needs of all students is foremost on this teacher's mind, and to accomplish it she puts her energy into planning.

EFFECTIVE CLASSROOM PLANNING

Classroom planning falls into two main categories: (1) physical environment, including books and supplies, and (2) curriculum content. The planning for these two categories constitutes some of the most intellectually intensive tasks a teacher can perform. Some teachers feel that their entire lives revolve around planning, but they acknowledge that these tasks provide them a tremendous creative outlet. Here teachers can be artists, not bound to a pattern but free to use their professional judgment experimentally, to decide what approach works best and when to use it. Such opportunities build teacher satisfaction and teacher self-esteem.

"Not surprisingly, there's a strong correlation between good management and good instruction," declares author Linda Shalaway. "Both require efficient organization and careful planning."

Planning the Physical Environment, Books, Supplies, and Materials

Furniture

- Arrange students' desks strategically.
- Arrange your desk with bookshelf and file cabinet close at hand.
- Designate shelves for student books and materials.
- Set aside tables for small groups or parent helpers.
- Plan storage areas for art and science supplies, etc.
- Provide space for students' lunches and backpacks.
- _____

Walls

- Designate a bulletin board for announcements, signs, rules, calendar, menu, birthdays, emergency procedures, etc.
- Designate a separate bulletin board for subject-area work.
- Allow one wall for students' original work.
- Save one area for you: personal items that make you smile.
- _____

Supplies and Materials

- Obtain all textbooks, kits, supplemental books, dictionaries, etc.
- Collect student literature and storybooks.

(Continued)

(Continued)

- Make available a variety of student writing paper.
- Collect a supply of construction and drawing paper.
- Make available for student use extra pencils, tissues, erasers, tape, stapler, paper clips, etc.
- Arrange A.V. equipment in user-ready areas.
- Designate trays for notes from home, returned homework, and finished work papers.

File Cabinet

- Assessment
- Faculty bulletins
- Homework ideas
- Correspondence from parents
- Parent notices
- Parent helpers
- Parent/teacher conferences
- Professional growth
- Poetry
- Holidays and seasons
- Literature units
- Math supplemental activities
- Language Arts supplements
- Art activities
- Plays, creative dramatics
- _____

Good Tips for Curriculum Planning

1. Set aside a regular daily time for planning.
2. Plan not to be a slave to your plans. Any good plan can be revised or augmented on the spot.
3. Determine what kids know about a subject before planning a unit or lesson. Often a few good questions will suffice.
4. Keep a file of "sponges" to soak up an extra few minutes.
5. Keep a "master plan book," organized with one double-spread page per week, for monthly appropriate ideas to use year after year.

6. Post a schedule of lessons for the day.

7. Plan transitions from one activity to another. (See Chapter 5.)

8. Always try to have materials ready for the next lesson.

9. Think through your lesson from beginning to end; imagine and visualize it in the classroom.

10. Use the 4E plan for lesson design:
    - Engage (to help students focus on the lesson)
    - Explain (to give directions and to model)
    - Explore (to provide guided practice and check for understanding)
    - Extend (to allow for independent practice)

11. Be creative. Slip in something fun. Include a surprise.

12. Use a variety of materials as well as hands-on manipulatives.

13. Make use of A.V. equipment whenever possible.

14. Plan effective use of aides, tutors, and parents.

15. Use seatwork as follow-up to material already covered.

16. Plan homework assignments that allow students to practice skills they've already learned.

ENHANCE YOUR ENVIRONMENT

Take a look around your classroom. Notice those things that reflect you—your personality, your creativity, and your needs. This classroom is yours. It's you! Within the constraints of school policy, try to make your room as comfortable as possible for your students and yourself. Take advantage of a sunny window: Hang some colored glass ornaments and bring in as many plants as fit the space. Bring in objects of art, posters, pillows, and rugs. Center one or two of your favorite paintings or photographs on a section of wall just for your own enjoyment, enhancing your space with your favorite things.

Warm inviting classrooms begin with the room's physical environment—the arrangement of desks and work tables, the attractiveness of walls and bulletin boards, the added "extra touch" of a caring teacher. Interesting items can actually motivate children, enhance learning, and reduce behavior problems.

Mr. McClurg is very aware of his room environment. Two thousand books, old and new, are arranged in his wonderful classroom library! An old flat-bottomed boat lined with pillows creates a reading nook. The bookshelves, some arranged at right angles to the wall, creating small reading areas, are made of warm, beautiful wood and often have incandescent lighting. There is a couch and chair in Mr. McClurg's room, along with a rug, growing plants, and a lamp.

Obviously this teacher bases much of his sixth-grade curriculum on literature. He regularly digs through used bookstores and junk shops to make living experiences of the literature he shares with his students. He truly brings stories alive, building history and other academia around each wonderful tale.

A BETTER CLASS BECAUSE OF THEIR OWNERSHIP

The warm and inviting physical environment described in the preceding section serves as a setting for the unique "family-style" climate created by Rob McClurg. In his class the 11-year-olds work together as an integral group to complete their assignments, plan and carry out projects, and have fun learning.

Managing a classroom is best achieved, in this teacher's experience, if everyone takes part. For example, all students work on the annual "Spell-a-thon" to raise money for classroom equipment. (Neighborhood sponsors pay a nickel for each correct word in a major spelling examination.) With the money kids have earned they have bought new encyclopedias, a VCR, a computer printer, and science equipment. "I do nothing for the children that they can do for themselves," this teacher declares. "This is one method of helping them become more responsible." He has found that along with increased responsibility comes increased self-esteem and a decrease in misbehavior. Here is problem prevention in action.

Cleaning and vacuuming their own classroom is a matter of pride to these students, so much so that they've relinquished their custodial time. By dividing up the jobs they keep their room clean and are proud of the results.

Teacher Note

He who fails to plan, plans to fail.

Kids with "attitudes"? Misbehavers? Yes, Mr. McClurg encounters his fair share of them. "There are always the kids," he points out, "who will push you to the limit, challenge authority, and try to get others to follow." But he lets them know that he and he alone is in charge. "Kids will always need firm guidance," he says. "It's up to the teacher to set limits, affirm students, and be constantly in charge."

The Message Is:

Good teaching occurs when carefully planned, effective strategies are employed by a skillful teacher with a warm, accepting attitude. An inviting environment sets the stage.

Figure 3.1   History on display.

Figure 3.2   A comfortable and inviting classroom.

PROMOTE A SENSE OF CLASS PRIDE

Wise teachers work to develop within their students a sense of class pride. "Our class is one of the best third grades in this school," these kids say. "We are proud that we follow school rules and that we're all doing our best."

You may encourage your class to choose a name for themselves and design a class banner. "Mr. Taylor's Tigers" is the banner over one third-grade classroom door. Other banners proclaim "Mrs. Rainey's Racers" and "Hansen's Hawks." You may also suggest that they create a class motto, such as that over the whiteboard in one classroom which reads, "I Don't Know How, But I'll Try!"

Students in Mrs. Heglie's class applaud each others' successes. She models respect and encouragement for all children, no matter their ability levels, and the students all smile with pride when an extra-hard worker succeeds.

"Yes, they've probably heard about you," says Mrs. Heglie when the class is notified of visitors coming to their room. "Now I suppose we'll have more and more visitors, since everybody knows how much you are learning!"

Try relaying a compliment to your class which was mentioned to you by another teacher, such as "Mrs. Narez noticed that you walked in a quiet line to the library and waited courteously to go in. She told me about it in the teachers' room, and I was so proud of you." Always bear in mind that the compliment need never have been given. If *you* see them walk nicely in line, you can just invent a compliment ostensibly from Mrs. Narez. Invented compliments from the principal are especially valuable!

Establishing and maintaining a sense of class pride will help students feel they belong to a great class and will contribute to a positive atmosphere. Have a discussion about class pride, why it is important and how it can be built. With the students acting as writers, editors, artists, and distributors, publish a class newspaper to keep everyone informed about class events and happenings.

A Sense of Class Pride

Name _____ Teacher _____

Think of something about your class that you are proud of every day for a week. Maybe it is something someone said or did. Be ready to share your ideas.

Monday _____

_____

_____

Tuesday _____

_____

_____

Wednesday _____

_____

_____

Thursday _____

_____

_____

Friday _____

_____

_____

Copyright © 2005 by Corwin Press. All rights reserved. Reprinted from *Teach More and Discipline Less: Preventing Problem Behaviors in the K–6 Classroom*, by Barbara Reider. Thousand Oaks, CA: Corwin Press, www.corwinpress.com. Reproduction authorized only for the local school site that has purchased this book.

The Message Is:

Classroom management is made easier when a sense of class pride has been fostered. The children intrinsically *want* to learn, *want* to behave, because they are proud of themselves as a group.

Teacher Note

Be sure to compliment your class within their hearing when the principal steps in. "Mr. Pogue, I want to recommend this class for the fourth grade! They have been working so hard in third-grade Math that I hardly have to teach at all!"

Figure 3.3   I don't know how, but I'll try.

Figure 3.4   Students here applaud each others' successes.

KIDS MUST RISK IN ORDER TO SUCCEED

All learning, declare the experienced teachers, requires a certain amount of risk taking. Students have to take risks every day in school, and it's our job as caring teachers to create a climate where it is safe to risk. And safe to fail.

But what kinds of assignments require risk taking? Think about it. To go up to the board and do a math problem in front of the class, to read a paragraph aloud, to recite a poem, all require taking risks. To write a report, to explain a math process to the group, even to raise a hand and take part in a discussion can be risks.

And what do children risk? Making a mistake, failure, embarrassment. They risk ridicule, put-downs, and at a deeper level their self-esteem.

We teachers know that for some children risking is easy. They answer, "Okay. I'll try it," when asked to go up to the board or required to demonstrate an experiment. For these children, confidence is high; they have plenty of self-esteem.

But some children are reluctant to try, afraid to take that risk, cautious about volunteering. They seem to have decided, "If I don't risk, I can't lose." These are the many who lack self-confidence. Teachers recognize these children and know that some will misbehave and some will withdraw, saying, "I can't." All are attempting to cover shaky self-esteem.

The Message Is:

Some children come to school with solid self-esteem, emanating from parent support and encouragement and from past successes, both academic and social. For them, taking academic risks is easy. Some come to school with low self-esteem, due to parent neglect and family problems, or from past failures, both academic and social. How can these children even be expected to risk?

MISTAKES: WONDERFUL OPPORTUNITIES TO LEARN

Teachers often wonder how they can help kids risk and thereby build confidence. The answer is to provide a climate which is safe enough for them to fail. To allow mistakes is to encourage learning, so the word must get out that in your class it's okay to make mistakes.

Make it safe for them to risk failure.

Mrs. Lowery realized that many of her sixth-grade students were so afraid of making mistakes that they were reluctant to join class discussions. Determined to meet the problem head-on, she initiated a discussion on the topic of failure. She began the discussion with easy questions relating to successes and failures when they were small children in school. As the discussion progressed, she encouraged her class to talk about the meaning of failure in their current lives, and finally brought them face to face with the social pressures and academic challenges of being in sixth grade. Soon their mistakes began to take on a less ominous look.

As a result of this discussion, Mrs. Lowery's class put together a list of six guidelines, titling the list "All About Mistakes."

Teacher Note

Providing a classroom climate in which it is safe to risk doesn't just happen with a snap of the fingers. It often involves finding the balance between the need for basic classroom control and the wish to be buddies with the kids.

Good teachers strive to find that balance.

1. It is okay to make mistakes.

2. An error is not a terror.

3. Don't make excuses for your mistakes.

4. Fix it. Don't defend it.

5. Learn from your mistakes.

6. Go back and read Number 1.

Students may be afraid to risk because they believe some old-fashioned ideas about making mistakes, including these common fallacies:

- You are stupid and a failure if you make mistakes.
- If you make a mistake, don't let people find out.
- Make up an excuse for every mistake you make.

According to Nelson, Lott, and Glenn, in *Positive Discipline in the Classroom*, teachers need to remind their students that we all make mistakes, and we all know people who have tried to cover up their mistakes and were then sorry. Most people admire those who admit their mistakes and apologize for problems they have caused.

The Message Is:

The greatest obstacle to learning is fear: fear of failure, fear of ridicule and put-downs, fear of appearing stupid, or even fear of appearing too smart. An effective teacher makes it possible for all children to make mistakes with impunity. Such a teacher knows that to remove fear is to invite kids to risk.

Figure 3.5   A teacher guides the group through a difficult lesson.

Mistakes
are for
correcting.

Figure 3.6   Peer teaching. (Who wants to study spelling alone?)

LOOK AT SOMETHING ANOTHER WAY

Ms. Gulas asks her students to stand up, look out the window, and tell her the first thing they see. She expects to get 30 answers, each one different: roof, four doors, a nest in the corner of the wall, some pillars, blue paint, a crack in the cement. Ms. Gulas says to them, "I heard 30 different answers. No two were alike, yet they all were correct, right?" She tells her students that in her class they will be looking for answers that are not all the same.

She then asks them, "What's half of 8?" warning that there are over 20 correct answers. She encourages them to think and keep thinking, and she gets a variety of answers:

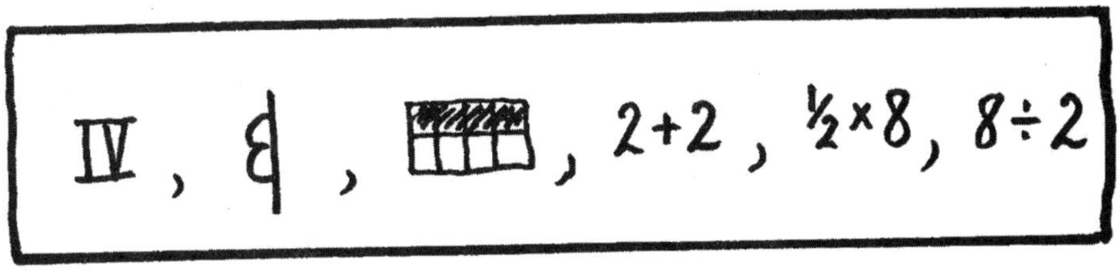

Figure 3.7   Different ways to say the same thing.

At each new suggestion, which the students write on the board, Ms. Gulas marvels at their cleverness in finding alternative answers. This teacher encourages her students to develop different perspectives and individual opinions.

She went on to explain, "When your children began Kindergarten, they may have learned this falsehood: There is only one right answer. Let them know that in your class there are many right answers. Allow them to come to you at any time with an alternative solution, and if they can justify it, give them credit."

The Message Is:

Exemplary teachers constantly challenge their students to see a new side to an issue and consider new possibilities. In this way teachers widen doors, broaden thinking, and promote creativity.

A TIME TO TALK, A TIME TO BE QUIET

Make sure your students are very clear about your expectations for the noise level in the classroom. For example, they should know precisely when it is okay to have conversations or discuss their work with others, and when it is not.

Once again, the key is consistency!

A bright-colored cardboard toucan is perched in the front corner of one primary classroom. From its beak hangs a two-sided sign which reads "NO TALK" on one side and "QUIET TALK" on the other. When the teacher hears inappropriate talking she simply says, "Excuse me. What does the toucan sign say right now?" A brief verbal reminder is all that is needed for most children, who are sometimes forgetful, aided by a toucan to help them remember. But it must be noted that it is *not* the toucan sign which prevents the students from talking. It is the teacher's consistency.

Quite often a teacher needs to interrupt the busily working class to deliver a message or give instructions. Sometimes the decibel level of the whole class is a little too high, and she needs immediate attention. Perhaps she will ring a small "freeze bell," and the students do just that—they freeze in their tracks, whatever they are doing. (Some love to be "caught" in comical acrobatic positions when they hear the bell.) Whatever method a teacher decides to use, she must remember one absolute: She must never speak until everyone is listening!

Procedures for Getting Attention

1. *Three soft tones on a xylophone.* "Bong, Bong, Bong," means stop and listen.

2. *The teacher's arm in the air; no words.* Students also raise their hands, indicating that they have noticed the signal and are ready to listen.

3. *Lights out briefly for total quiet and attention.* Students generally take a deep breath during their moment in the dark, time to relax and listen to a message.

4. *Five-minute timer, set by the teacher.* Children know they have 5 minutes to finish work, put materials away, look at the teacher, and show her they're ready.

5. *"Give me five," pronounced by the teacher.* This signals students to mentally review their five steps for quiet: (1) eyes on speaker; (2) mouth quiet; (3) ears listening; (4) hands free; (5) sitting still.

The Message Is:

The most disturbing problem to teachers is probably the long-standing and still-annoying issue of students talking when they should be working or listening. Therefore, it is wise to introduce a visual *and* an auditory reminder on the very first day, to be practiced, reviewed, and consistently enforced.

CAPTAIN OF THE WEEK

Many teachers know the wisdom of assigning various classroom responsibilities to one class leader, who keeps the position for one week. The leader is chosen never by popular vote, but simply by drawing a name out of a basket, ensuring absolute fairness. It is considered a great honor to hold this position.

There are various creative titles for these prestigious leaders, such as Head Honcho, Star of the Week, VIP (Very Important Person), Eager Eagle, Big Apple, Superkid, and Captain of the Week.

Since the position is such a big responsibility, the duties of the Captain of the Week should be a major topic of discussion at the beginning of the year. What qualities should a good leader have? For what jobs will he be responsible? After the discussion, you and your class can make a list of duties that might include

- Pass out paper and other materials
- Lead the line to computer class or music
- Straighten library shelves
- Monitor P.E. equipment
- Decorate bulletin boards
- Excuse class for recess and lunch
- Deliver messages

As an alternative to one main leader, some teachers institute a "job program" available to students who apply for the jobs. The purpose, of course, is to promote responsibility and the self-discipline required to complete the tasks they agree to do. The job titles and descriptions are posted, the students fill in applications, and they are hired for a 2- to 4-week period. Job titles may include

- Messenger
- File clerk
- Dismissal sergeant
- Librarian
- Paper monitor
- Equipment manager (P.E.)
- Line leader

NOTHING LIKE A GOOD LAUGH!

A sense of humor is a necessity in the classroom. Surely Mary Poole must have been referring to the everyday hardworking teacher when she observed, "He who laughs, lasts." And Mary McKeown must see the value of a good laugh when she suggests these whimsical strategies.

Humor Lightens the Day

If the kids are struggling through a math lesson and just can't get the new concept, stop them! Say, "Boys and girls, I have the answer to your math problems! It's the fault of the pencils! I am now handing you a new pencil, a *math pencil.* Now you'll all be able to get this work finished!"

Humor Bonds the Students and Teacher

When the class has had a successful morning, say to them, "Whatever you had for breakfast, eat that every morning for the rest of your life!"

Humor Defuses a Tense Situation

A pencil flies out of a student's hand and sails across the room. The children gasp, expecting your anger. Say, "Aha! Throwing things at the teacher! John, you must go to bed with no supper for six nights!"

Humor Causes Kids to Stop, Blink, and Laugh

When you open a note from a parent, read it aloud and purposefully read it *wrong:* "Billy had a temper tantrum last night because he didn't have enough homework. Please give him 200 spelling words tonight!" And after they stop, blink, and laugh, tell Billy he absolutely may NOT have more homework tonight!

Humor Puts the Students at Ease

To lighten the day and put students at ease, tell a good joke. Make it silly enough for all of the gigglers in your class. Once in a while, tape an amusing cartoon on the door to encourage a chuckle. Plan a funny hat day or a funny poem day, where everyone may participate.

ROUNDUP OF CHAPTER 3

1. Teaching requires both a caring attitude and specific strategies.

2. Planning is a major key to professional success.

3. Make your classroom environment feel comfortable and inviting.

4. Find ways that your students can feel ownership in their classroom.

5. Build a sense of class pride in as many ways as possible.

6. Remember that risking is difficult for some children.

7. Let it be okay for kids to make mistakes.

8. Let kids know that in your class different opinions and perspectives are encouraged.

9. Use a visual reminder in the classroom for talking and quiet time.

10. Consider using a special signal to get students' attention.

11. Build responsibility in many ways, including choosing a leader of the week.

12. Remember the wonderful value of a sense of humor.

4 Promote a Feeling of Cohesiveness

GROUPING FOR COOPERATION

The introduction of this book defines the book's focus as one of prevention rather than the handling of misbehavior. Its purpose is to prevent discipline problems before they start by skillfully managing the environment. Chapters 1, 2, and 3 describe proven methods and strategies for not only creating the environment, but also for getting to know kids and building trust and rapport.

Chapter 4 takes the teacher one step farther. Now you will build a sense of community within your class through various types of groupings. You'll begin with the large group—your entire class—engaged in a variety of discussions and activities, and when you determine students are ready, you will set up small groups with various requirements and assignments.

A special spirit of community doesn't just happen by putting children in groups, however, or by leading them in discussions and activities. Building a sense of community will be accomplished over a period of time, by a teacher who is dedicated to creating a positive learning environment. It begins by ensuring inclusion for every child and proceeds to a full feeling of cohesiveness for all class members. This chapter presents strategies for building a sense of community, and in so doing, preventing discipline problems before they start.

COMMUNITY CIRCLE: SIMPLE BUT POWERFUL

Without a clear feeling of group identity, a caring classroom is an illusion. One excellent method for building this identity among your students is to meet frequently in Community Circles. These simple group discussions are popular with kids because they are non-threatening, and are valuable to teachers because they are effective in promoting inclusion and class cohesion. The directions are as follows:

Seat your students and yourself in a circle on the floor, all of you sitting cross-legged. Place your hand on your neighbor's knee (or shoulder, if you prefer) and say, "This is my friend Eric." Keep your hand on Eric's knee as he introduces his neighbor, "This is my friend Karen." Proceed around the circle, letting each child introduce his neighbor and keeping a hand on a knee. Watch as they all smile and sit a little taller when they are introduced. Notice the feeling of cohesiveness that is apparent when all hands are on knees around the circle and all children have been introduced. (This feeling explains why this activity is sometimes referred to as "Magic Circle.") Say to them, "Look at all these smiles! We *are* a wonderful class! Now put your hands in your laps and let's begin."

That was Part One of a simple community circle discussion. You have already begun to set a tone of inclusion and cohesion. Now announce your "sentence starter" for the day, which will begin Part Two. An easy example of a sentence starter is, "In my free time I like to. . . ." Give the students a few moments to think about their responses to the topic, and then take your turn first by finishing the sentence. Proceed around the circle as before, with everyone taking a turn to complete the sentence.

Two rules apply, and should be explained before you begin. Rule number one: *Thumbs-up for everyone.* All of you will give a thumbs-up signal to each participant as he finishes. Rule number two: *Right to pass.* Anyone not wishing to take a turn may simply say "Pass," and he receives a thumbs-up also.

Teacher Note

Train yourself to react to children's comments with *only a smile.* If you enthusiastically say "Good job!" to one child you'll have to say it 23 more times! Model smiles and thumbs-up for everyone, and the class will soon follow suit.

The Message Is:

A community circle discussion, easy to conduct, is indeed very powerful! It is a self-esteem builder. It promotes self-awareness. (Some children have never spoken so openly about their feelings.) It promotes respect for others. (Notice that everyone's opinion counts.) It builds self-confidence. (Even the shy child can feel safe enough in this circle to make a contribution and feel included.)

Figure 4.1   Young students feel comfortable in their community circle.

Figure 4.2   With this ancient rifle I can pretend. . . .

Sentence Starters

1. I'm really good at. . . .
2. It's easy for me to. . . .
3. It's hard for me to. . . .
4. I get scared when. . . .
5. I'm embarrassed when. . . .
6. It bugs me when. . . .
7. I'm happy when. . . .
8. I feel sad when. . . .
9. I get angry when. . . .
10. Someday I hope. . . .
11. Next year I want to. . . .
12. I'd like to learn to. . . .
13. In my free time I. . . .
14. On weekends I like to. . . .
15. I wish my mom would. . . .
16. I wish my teacher would. . . .
17. I don't like it when. . . .
18. I'd like to ask my teacher. . . .
19. I'd like to ask the principal. . . .
20. If I were the teacher, I. . . .
21. My favorite weather is. . . .
22. Rain makes me feel. . . .
23. Sunshine makes me feel. . . .
24. If I were an animal, I'd be a. . . .
25. When I grow up I. . . .
26. If I ruled the world. . . .

INCIDENTAL DISCUSSIONS AS PROBLEM SOLVERS

Occasionally during the day in a classroom full of lively kids, a topic comes up "out of the blue," and you realize it's time for an Incidental Discussion. Especially if you know that the subject is emotionally charged and the class will benefit by discussing it immediately, you will squeeze a little time into your schedule. Stop everything and devote a few minutes to the issue.

Teacher Note

Class discussions are also useful to stimulate thought and encourage students to re-examine their attitudes.

Example: An announcement has just been made by the principal. There has been a change in plans. Instead of the entire class only a selected few children will be allowed to attend the assembly program this afternoon. Everyone is upset, those excluded as well as those allowed to go. "It's not fair," they say. "We all prepared for this program." *This is the time for an incidental discussion.*

Example: During recess someone came into your classroom and messed up the science experiment your class has on display. Everyone is upset. *This is the time for an incidental discussion.*

The Message Is:

Class discussions, either planned or incidental, are prime times for building class cohesiveness. Recognize these as opportunities for your students to pull together toward a common goal, solve a problem, make a plan, or organize a project.

Self-Esteeming Civil Rights

I have a right to hear and be heard in this classroom.

This means that others will speak respectfully and listen attentively while I have a turn to talk.

I have a right to be myself in this classroom.

This means that others will applaud my individuality—my personal characteristics and my opinions.

*I have a right to be happy and to be
treated with compassion in this classroom.*

This means that others will treat me with honor and respect as an important member of this class.

Teacher Tips for Discussions

1. Be careful to include all students in class discussions. Standing at the front of the room, a teacher tends to call on children at the back of the room, on her far right or far left, and not those up near the front. Try to resist this tendency.

2. Studies indicate that teachers call on boys more often than girls, especially boys who do not sit and wait patiently for a turn. Teachers also tend to call on students whom they feel will know the "right answer." For these reasons we must take special care to call on *all* students.

3. Train yourself to accept each comment in a discussion in a noncommittal way. To encourage participation, take care not to evaluate opinions by (a) making judgmental comments or (b) showing judgmental facial expressions.

4. Always bear in mind the confidence that a child gains when he states his opinion before a group. In life there are many opportunities to speak for oneself. The more we encourage children to do so, the more we prepare them for life outside school.

5. Respect the personal opinions of everyone. If a child gives an opinion contrary to yours or that of the general public, his opinion must nevertheless be considered worthy. When Cody declares, "It's a waste of money to send rockets into space," accept his opinion. Ask for other comments on the subject. Usually the pros and cons will evolve.

6. Allow the student to talk on a subject that might be considered personal if you see that it is beneficial to him. Let students express themselves.

7. Students need to have time set aside to sit down together to review what happened in class yesterday, make decisions, solve problems, and plan events. You, the teacher, must decide at each moment during the discussion whether to sit back or step in. From these sessions students will come to believe that their decisions matter.

8. The important thing is to learn about each other as individuals and slowly come to feel a part of an "us"!

A SCHEDULED CLASSROOM MEETING

Many teachers see the advantages of scheduling a more formal class discussion once or twice a week. These discussions, called Classroom Meetings, usually have a definite purpose, such as planning an event, examining a problem, or considering an issue brought up by the teacher. They are useful strategies for stimulating thought and encouraging students to examine their attitudes and voice their opinions.

> Learning happens in a group. . . . It's a social phenomenon.

The teacher and students seat themselves on chairs arranged in a circle. This arrangement ensures that everyone can see and hear each other and all will feel a sense of equality. Years of experience have taught veteran teachers that a circle is by far the most effective arrangement. Students are more encouraged to respond to each other rather than dialogue with the teacher if they can see each other. Although monitors can be appointed to arrange the chairs in advance, students can easily push their own chairs into a circle in a very short time. It just takes a little practice to make this run smoothly.

The classroom meeting always begins with compliments, which, with your help and example, children will learn to offer each other. Compliments start the meeting on a positive note, since it boosts everyone's self-esteem both to give a word of praise and to hear something nice said about them. And of course, each compliment deserves a thank you.

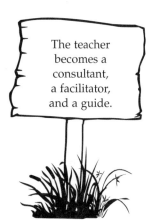

The teacher becomes a consultant, a facilitator, and a guide.

Examples of simple and heartfelt compliments that kids make are: "Tricia, I appreciate the book you brought in for me." "Jack, you came up with a good plan at recess." "I appreciated it when Miguel helped me in math." Compliments are encouraged but never mandatory.

After compliments, you, the teacher, are in charge of introducing the topic for the meeting. Yours is the role of moderator; you generally refrain from offering your opinion. At times the topic is a problem that needs to be solved or a plan that must be set up. But often you will begin the meeting with a question intended to pique the interest of your class. (Several such questions are suggested below.) Discussion follows, with students raising their hands to speak, and you, the teacher, making every effort to keep the group focused on the topic.

In his book, *Schools Without Failure*, William Glasser tells of classroom meetings he has initiated with this, his favorite question: "Suppose someone gave me two tickets to Disneyland and said I should award them to two children in this class. To whom should I give the tickets?" Glasser reports that some interesting discussions have been instigated with this question. Children are always very concerned with making decisions fairly and democratically; therefore, they typically make carefully considered suggestions. (The most common solution is to give the tickets to one good student and one poor student, neither of whom has ever been to Disneyland. To children, this is the most fair solution.)

Teacher Note

Traditional methods of conducting discussions are teacher-centered, with the teacher at the front asking questions and pointing out concepts, meanwhile maintaining discipline. But real learning happens in a circle. Attention then focuses on the task, not the teacher.

Topics for Classroom Meetings

1. Should you do your homework yourself, or should your parents help you? How much help should a parent give? How does homework build a sense of responsibility?

2. What is a friend? How do you choose your friends? Is it good to have a lot of friends or just a few? What do friends do to keep the friendship going? Do friendships end, or do we keep friendships forever?

3. How much work should you do around the house? Should boys do more work? What kind of work should girls do? Should it be different from boys' work? Should you be paid for work you do at home, or should you donate your time as a contribution to the household?

4. What is the use of going to college? Is college more important today than it was years ago? Should students work their way through college? How much should parents give up to put a student through college? Should you decide whether you are going, or should parents decide?

5. What can we do with the child who doesn't behave? Should we keep him out of games? Why do you think kids act that way? What do you think about a kid who always has to be the center of attention in class?

6. Do teenagers dress differently today than they used to? Why do they wear rings in their ears and noses? Do teenagers, who seem so nonconforming, conform in any way? Is there anyone here who doesn't conform? What will you wear and do when you're a teenager?

7. Who would you like to be if you could wake up tomorrow and be someone else? The teacher? The principal? How would you treat children if you were the teacher? How would you treat teachers if you were the principal? What would you do if you were a policeman?

8. How would your life be different if you were a black person or a white person? If you woke up a different race or color, how would it be? If all white people were black and all black people were white, how would it make a difference in your neighborhood?

Several of the topic questions presented in the list were adapted from the aforementioned book by William Glasser. They target problems which are important to children of all ages, problems such as friendship, life in school, and growing up. As a teacher, you can easily generate questions simply by being aware of your students' interests and readiness. Questions can center around the *importance* of such things as

- Books
- Education
- Laws
- Doctors
- The environment

Questions can also be generated by the *problems* of

- Ecology
- Overcrowded cities
- Television
- Divorce
- Delinquency

Obviously subject matter for classroom meetings is limitless. Anything of interest is a possibility. Children need to talk about what they are learning, why it is important, and how it is connected to their lives. There may be few more useful discussions than a sustained discussion following someone's challenge: "Why do we hafta do this stuff?"

The Message Is:

Children are interested in the world outside their neighborhoods and their towns. They are willing to discuss worldly ideas once they believe the discussion is worthwhile, that everyone gets to participate, and that others are listening to them. The discussions promote involvement and raise self-esteem when they are relevant, thought-provoking, and *fun.*

Figure 4.3   Fifth graders engage in a discussion about slaves who sabotaged their
masters.

KIDS SUGGEST TOPICS FOR DISCUSSION

In many classrooms the students are encouraged to suggest topics for
the agenda, further adding to their sense of
class connectedness. When students participate in classroom meetings, and also initiate
the topics, they find that they can make a difference and feel a sense of ownership in their
classroom. They learn that their opinions matter to others; their contributions are valued.

You may wish to set out a clipboard
with paper labeled "CLASSROOM MEETING
AGENDA." In this way you can encourage
students to suggest topics or problems they
want discussed. Instruct them to write their
names on the agenda, and mention their
topics in one or two words. Their topics or
problems will then be discussed during a
scheduled classroom meeting. Expect your
students to suggest topics such as

Teacher Note

Ground rules for classroom
meetings should be
reviewed each time a
meeting is held. The
ground rules all stress
mutual respect:

1. One person talks
   at a time.
2. Listen when others
   speak.
3. No put-downs
   allowed.

Every opinion counts!

- A party on the last day before Christmas
- Bigger kids causing trouble on the playground
- "Secret pals" in other classrooms
- What to do about a kid acting like a bully

Encourage children who are reluctant to contribute by saying, "Cameron, you have been listening so intently; I'm sure you have an idea that I'd like to hear."

The Message Is:

Classroom meetings are welcomed with enthusiasm by students of all ages. They will be as successful as the imagination, skill, and conviction of the teacher who runs them.

ACTIVITIES TO BUILD A FEELING OF BELONGING

Children who share experiences and learn about each other develop a closeness with one another. Besides discussions, there are a variety of whole-group activities which build inclusion and cohesion, and have as their goal a positive feeling of belonging. The following are a few examples.

All in the Family

Ask students to sit in groups around the room according to their birth order in the family: oldest, in-betweens, youngest, only child. Write these questions on the board for all groups to discuss: (1) How does it feel to be (oldest)? (2) What responsibilities do you have? (3) What advantages do you have?

Then merge two groups together and have them discuss: (1) Who do you think has more power in the family? (2) Who gets the attention, and how do they get it?

Seated back in their desks after these discussions, ask the class what they learned by this activity. "Which comments surprised you? Did you feel a common bond with those in your own group?"

Other People's Shoes

Ask students to write on a card one secret hope that they may have. Tell them not to write their names, but to drop their cards in a paper bag in the center of the room, then sit in a large circle for this activity. Now have each participant draw out a secret hope card (making sure they don't get their own). Ask each of them to read the card and put themselves in the other person's shoes. Encourage them to imagine how it feels to have this secret hope.

Then ask them to tell the others in the circle what it is they wish will come true.

Try this activity another day, writing about secret fears or concerns.

Sports Heroes

Give each student a large piece of paper, a felt marker, and some masking tape. Ask each one to print the following words at the top of the paper: "I like (a favorite sports hero) because. . . ." Then have them all tape their papers on their own backs. Have them stand around so others can write on their "capes." After all have written, ask students to sit in a circle and read their papers out loud.

Also try this activity with famous people from history or literature, or maybe with the students' own names.

What's in My Name

On the night before you do this activity, have the students write the answers to these questions at home:

1. Why did your parents choose your name?

2. If you were named for someone, who was it?

3. What nicknames do you have; how did you get them?

4. Do you like your name? Why or why not?

5. If you could choose another name, what would it be?

After all students have brought in their "homework" assignments, sit in a circle to read over each of the questions and share answers. Ask if they noticed similarities in how names were chosen, or ask how they feel about their nicknames; discuss the origin of family names.

Students frequently come to school with biases and social prejudice, but cooperative activities such as the four just described can help overcome them. Research tells us that racial and gender relations improve in classrooms where students interact cooperatively to meet specific teacher-assigned goals.

Three concepts of cooperation to be consistently promoted are

- Everyone gets to participate.
- Everyone wins.
- The better we work together, the more fun we have.

Good teachers stress social responsibility not only by discussions and cooperative games, but through peer tutoring, art projects, drama experiences, and academic work in teams. Small cooperative group experiences will be discussed later in this chapter.

KIDS DISCUSS MISBEHAVIOR

Ms. Davis, a fourth-grade teacher, regularly schedules classroom meetings with her students. Early in the school year, when she feels a positive rapport has begun to develop, she uses a classroom meeting to address the subject of misbehavior. She says to her class, "Suppose that one day you found yourself acting in a way you weren't proud of. Perhaps you hurt someone's feelings or shouted at the teacher. How would you want the rest of the class to help you?" The class spends a bit of time discussing this question, and then Penny Davis asks, "What if someone else acted that way? How could we help that person?"

A lengthy discussion always follows the introduction of this topic, its success due partly to the students' opportunity to personalize the issue. Some of the fourth-grade comments might be, "Maybe the girl thinks nobody likes her." "Maybe she's doing it for attention." "We could all make a pact to be nicer to the person." "We should put it on the agenda and have a discussion about it."

This teacher wants her class to think about misbehavior in terms of prevention, which is precisely why she works on building a cooperative environment and conducts activities like those found in this book. She knows that all kids have the potential to work together to help a misbehaver. But she also knows that all kids have the potential to misbehave! So she encourages them to talk about it, while helping them to view misbehavior as an indication that a child needs help.

Ms. Davis' strategy for problem prevention is excellent. She deflects a potential stewpot full of problems by addressing the issue early on.

The Message Is:

Children who are inclined to look at behavior in a constructive way are found in a cohesive classroom. Their reaction is likely to be "How can we solve this problem together?" rather than to suggest a punishment.

Large- and Small-Group Work

	Grouping Technique	To Be Used When . . .	Scheduling
Incidental Discussion	Total group; children remain at their desks	. . . a topic of imminent interest presents itself.	Adjust schedule to make time for discussion.
Classroom Meeting With Teacher Agenda	Total group, including teacher, seated in large circle of chairs	. . . plans or procedures need to be discussed. . . . the teacher presents an issue.	Scheduled weekly at teacher's discretion.
Classroom Meeting With Student Agenda	Total group, including teacher, seated in large circle of chairs	. . . students have a topic or issue to be discussed.	Scheduled according to student need or interest.
Cooperative Learning Group Meetings	Small groups of 5 or 6 students at tables or desk clusters	. . . the teacher assigns team activities.	According to a once- or twice-weekly set schedule.

READY TO WORK IN SMALL COOPERATIVE GROUPS

By now your students have taken part in many whole-group cooperative activities programmed to build a sense of community. They have taken part daily in News and Sharing time, have helped set their own rules, have chosen a name for their class, and have been a part of various class discussions and activities. As their teacher, you have arranged these activities as integral elements of your classroom management strategy because you know the preventive power of a positive class climate. Students now feel free to take risks and make mistakes.

With this background of experiences, the students are ready to work in small cooperative learning groups for a part of each day. Research shows that students who work successfully in small groups will show an increase in

> **Teacher Note**
>
> Hundreds of studies in American social psychology show that cooperative learning leads to higher achievement for all students. Students' responsibility for helping each other with assignments and problems also lightens the teacher's task of classroom management.

- Problem-solving skills
- Retention of knowledge
- Responsible behavior
- Racial tolerance
- Leadership skills
- Creativity
- Self-esteem
- Positive peer relationships

Each student in a group will be responsible not only for his own learning but the learning of his fellow group members. They will be working toward a common goal and their success will be dependent upon their working interdependently. All will soon discover that a group of students who care for and are committed to each other will achieve more quickly and efficiently than if each were to attempt the task alone. But each child needs to discover this truth for himself.

The activities that the groups will engage in generally fall into two categories: (1) planning, problem solving, and maintaining an environment of positive support for each other, and (2) working cooperatively to learn academic content.

The Message Is:

Cooperative learning is a bonus for children's education. It fosters social skills, including leadership, seeking and giving help, decision making, and conflict management. All of these are skills which they will need to be successful in later life. Everyone wins: the students, the teachers, the parents, and the community in which they live.

Figure 4.4   Each group member is responsible for one-fifth of the research.

Cooperative learning
is two things:

1. Learning to
    cooperate
2. Cooperating
    to learn

Figure 4.5   The teacher is free to consult with each group as
needed.

SETTING THE STAGE

With a little thought and planning, you can make up a list of five or six
groups in your classroom. Try to assign no more than five children to a
group, equally distributing the boys and girls, as well as the "leader"
types, the high and low achievers, and the potential disrupters.

Then, on a day when you determine the children are ready, and you have made the necessary preparations, you will decide to go into *small-group mode.* Be sure to allow a good hour for this special organizational event.

An exciting way for children to discover who is in which group is for you to prepare "people puzzles." (See Figure 4.8.) For each group, cut a square poster board into five puzzle-shaped pieces, and write one of the five names on each piece. (Be sure to cut each puzzle separately so no two are alike.) When all are prepared, hide them around the room during lunch or recess.

When the children come in, tell them that you believe they are now responsible enough to handle themselves in small groups. Instruct them to search around the room for their names and to fit their puzzle pieces together in order to form new learning teams. When all the puzzles are together, congratulate the participants. Tell them, "You will work together as a team for an hour or so every day, and I think you'll be surprised how much you can accomplish when everyone pulls together." Explain that after one month you all may decide to change the groups.

The children will need to move their desks each day so they can sit together as teams. Perhaps you will wish to make some changes in your permanent seating arrangement to enable them to move quickly into their groups. Decide upon a signal that you will give when you want to form groups. And finally, review the rules to be used in group work, which are basically those they learned for classroom meetings: (1) One person talks at a time. (2) Listen when others speak. (3) No put-downs allowed. Some teachers display these rules on colored paper balloons in their classrooms.

PRACTICE WORKING TOGETHER IN GROUPS

"Kids learn amazingly well in small groups," says third-grade teacher Ann Harry. But she cautions against forming groups so the more capable students always seem to serve as tutors to the less able learners, thereby missing the challenge of their intellectual peers. She points out, "The key is to organize your learning teams so that all students are responsible for their own learning and behavior." Mrs. Harry continues with this advice: "Don't assume that they know at first how to work in groups. You have to begin slowly, and teach them."

Immediately after your groups have been formed you will lead them in an activity which builds inclusion so they can become familiar with each other. The following activity is simple, but it does the job and takes very little time.

Wishful Thinking

1. Ask the teams to sit in small circles.

2. Instruct them each to make a brief statement going around the circle, beginning with "I wish. . . ." Statements can be about school, vacations, their personal life, etc.

3. Let them go around the circle three times, while all others listen courteously.

4. When all groups are finished, ask how they felt about the activity, and whether all of their team members followed the rules.

The Message Is:

The members of the groups will bond together, peer teaching will take place, and everyone will work for the good of the team instead of competing with one another. They may get to work in their group every day throughout an entire unit of study, or for just one specific activity.

Figure 4.6   Rules listed on balloons.

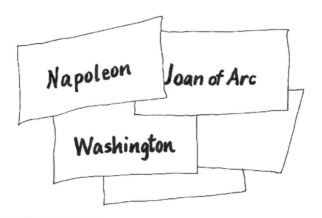

Figure 4.7 History exercise.

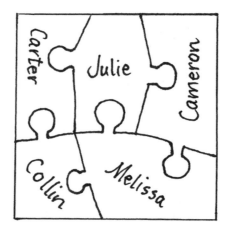

Figure 4.8 People puzzle.

Most areas of the curriculum that you usually teach can easily be integrated into the cooperative learning group process. Math, science, history, literature, and art can be studied in groups. The following is an example of a small-group lesson in history.

History

Meet Charles Lindbergh

Instructions:

1. Write on cards the names of six historical characters with whom your students are somewhat familiar. Pass out one card to a team.

2. Allow teams 20 minutes to look up information and write down as much as they can about their person.

3. Ask each team to choose one person to "be" the historical character. This person will sign his or her "name" on the board and take a seat at the front of the room flanked by the four or five other team members.

4. In this way allow each character to tell the class about his or her prominence in history and team members to help field questions from the class.

5. Applaud loudly for each character's performance.

Literature and Phonics

What Will Happen Next?

Instructions:

1. The teacher reads a story, stopping at an interesting or suspenseful part.

2. Have each group decide what they think will happen next.

3. Let them write or draw their story ending.

4. Ask the groups to present their versions of the story ending to the entire class.

5. Lead applause for each group.

Phonic Inchworms*

Instructions:

1. Give each team six colored paper circles, 5 inches in diameter.

2. Following a discussion of consonant blend sounds, such as *kl*, *sk*, and *fr*, assign one blend to each team member.

3. Ask each team member to write three words on his circle which begins with his sound. Encourage them to help each other.

4. Have the team draw a "worm face" on the sixth circle, and glue or staple their "worm parts" together into a long inchworm.

5. Invite all teams to display their worms on the board.

NOTE: *This method may also be used for math and reading vocabulary.

Tips for Teams

1. Try to program small-group work at a specific time each day.

2. Use a signal for team members to arrange their desks.

3. Briefly review the rules for team conduct each day.

4. Explain the task or activity of the day, giving directions clearly or writing the steps on the board.

5. Announce a time for the tasks to be finished.

6. Remind students to ask their team members, not the teacher, when they have a question, and to be ready to help a buddy when asked.

7. All members of the group share leadership responsibilities. Everyone does his job and everyone benefits.

8. Consider yourself the team consultant. Move about among the groups to observe. Help only if needed.

9. When work is finished, allow all class members to discuss and reflect upon their success as team players. Have group members report as needed.

TEAMS IN COMPETITION

Some teachers set up a program of competition between their teams as a classroom management tool, believing that children have a natural interest in competing. The program operates by peer pressure, as students police each other's work habits and adherence to rules. The philosophy behind such a program is not universal by any means, and the following idea is not intended to be a recommendation.

Allow your teams to choose names for themselves, and then display the team names on a permanent chart in your room. Explain to your class that each team can earn points, which you will tally during the day. Points will be awarded for such things as

- Good behavior
- Walking in quietly and settling down to work
- Following directions
- Participation in activities

- A compliment from the principal
- A positive comment by another teacher
- Following rules in the library
- Cleaning up their area

Remind the students that poor group behavior, failure to follow directions, or disrupting the class can result in a loss of points for a team. Keep a tally of points throughout the morning, and allow the winning team to be excused first for lunch. Follow the same procedure in the afternoon.

Keep in mind the two main goals of grouping your students, which are to promote a sense of community and to prevent discipline problems.

ROUNDUP OF CHAPTER 4

1. Never fail to recognize the power of a simple community circle.

2. Model respect for all students and their opinions.

3. Allow an imminent problem to be settled right now with an incidental discussion.

4. Be aware of the tendency to exclude certain children in discussions.

5. Train yourself to accept all opinions in a discussion in a noncommittal way.

6. Hold classroom meetings to discuss school and social problems of importance to your students.

7. Encourage children to suggest topics for discussion.

8. Use various total group activities to promote inclusion and cohesiveness.

9. Lead discussions about misbehavior to help children understand why people break rules.

10. Introduce small cooperative learning groups when you *and* the students are ready for it.

11. Organize your small groups with great care, and walk them through the basics of organization.

12. Remember, your job is to observe and consult. The students are busy becoming autonomous. You must be patient and let them work through the process.

5 Minimize Problems With Proven Techniques

THE ART OF ASKING GOOD QUESTIONS

Research tells us that in a regular classroom, two-thirds of the class time is spent in verbal interaction, two-thirds of the verbal interaction is composed of teacher talk, and two-thirds of teacher talk is asking questions. Either good teaching or poor teaching will take place, depending on the quality of the interaction between teacher and student; therefore, a teacher's questioning skills are of great importance.

Too often we ask questions which require simple recall of facts. "How many boats reached the shore?" "Where did the explorers build their camp?" "What happened next?" From experienced teachers we can discover the various kinds of questions to ask, as well as tips on their delivery and, just as important, skillful ways of responding to comments made by children.

Questions are divided into three levels of difficulty, and the best teaching takes place when all three levels are used:

1. "Recall" questions

2. "Why" questions

3. "What if" questions

"Recall" questions require students to recite from memory, most commonly to elicit facts about something they have already learned. They help teachers determine what students have absorbed, and can also be used as an anticipatory set, to bring attention to a new topic.

"Why" questions ask students to compare or classify, or offer an opinion. For example, "Why do we say a map is like a recipe?" "Why do you think the two nations fought one another?" Also in this category is, "How do you know that?"

"What if" questions require the highest level of thinking skills, challenging students to imagine or predict. For example, "What do you think will happen if the father wolf never comes back to the cubs?" "What if rainfall amounts fall to dangerous levels?" "What if the Spanish monks had turned back on their trail north from Mexico?"

Questioning Suggestions

- It is wise to limit the use of recall questions as well as those which require only a Yes or No answer. Rather, challenge your students to higher levels of thinking by planning your questioning strategies carefully, using Level 2 and 3 questions.
- When a student responds, occasionally say, "Yes, but tell me why." This tells you whether he knows more than the basic brief answer and allows him to process his information aloud.
- Pause after asking a question, perhaps 3 to 5 seconds. A pause indicates that the question is meant for everyone, not just one or two quick thinkers. It enables slow thinkers to participate and gives everyone time to think carefully and answer with confidence.
- When students answer, make eye contact and listen to what they say.
- Avoid calling on a student before asking your question, which generally causes the other students not to listen. Avoid repeating students' answers, which allows the students to listen only to the teacher.
- Paraphrase a child's response, or ask him to clarify, because this tells him "I value what you say."
- Occasionally follow up a child's response with, "How did you come up with your answer?" This helps the student who couldn't answer the question to better understand.
- Ask questions that can sometimes be answered silently, or in writing, not just orally.

- Be accepting and nonjudgmental about children's responses. Neither praise nor criticize. Avoid words such as *right, wrong, good, bad, better*, and *worse*. Always encourage a child to think, "My opinions are worthy."
- If a child gives an answer that is obviously wrong, do your best to help him save face. If you ask for the definition of gravity and he says, "when something falls from a high place," say to him, "You're on the right track. But what does gravity have to do with it?"
- Encourage creativity and imagination with your questions. Ask students to take the part of someone else with, "How did the grandfather feel?" Or ask divergent questions such as, "How is an airplane like a book?" "How is a frog like a tree?" Celebrate diversity. Applaud imagination. "Too often, in attempting to teach children the 'right' answers, it's easy to squelch their imaginations," proclaims Linda Shalaway, author of *Learning to Teach*. "Don't forget to give them the room they need to develop an important intellectual tool—their imaginations."

One final point on questioning techniques is a warning about negative remarks made by other children, especially when a child makes a mistake. Unfortunately put-down remarks are a basic form of communication among children these days, but put-downs not only damage self-esteem, they also lower the level of trust within a group. As teachers we must constantly challenge the students themselves to prohibit negative remarks. Moreover, we must continually model positive comments which show acceptance. "Interesting point of view, Lisa." " Dave, I can tell you've given that a lot of thought." Once again, we can all work together to respect the opinions of everyone in our classroom community.

No
put-downs
allowed.

Figure 5.1   If half of the students raise a hand to respond, this teacher knows his question is appropriate.

Begin
questions with:

• Who
  remembers . . .
• Why . . .
• What if . . .

Figure 5.2   Short writing prompts, changed weekly, are used as transition activities.

The Message Is:

Questioning techniques are of paramount importance. Here is where teachers are the decisive elements in the classroom. Here is when their personal approach creates the climate, and their moods make the weather. For it is here that teachers are completely in charge.

ORCHESTRATE SMOOTH TRANSITIONS

The most likely occasions for *chaos* to occur during your teaching day are the moments when students are transitioning from one activity to another; therefore, one of the biggest payoffs for closely maintained standard procedures are smooth transitions. If you are an elementary teacher, there will be a transition from math to recess, from an individual desk activity to group work, or from lunch to a science lesson. If you teach at a departmentalized level, transitions are compounded by changing periods every 50 minutes or so. How you handle these few minutes, as one activity ends and another begins, spells the difference between chaos and order.

Transitions need to be *engineered,* whether they are one- or two-step directions or need to be taught as standard procedures. This means that you must carefully explain what you expect and how you expect it to be accomplished. Insist that it be done that way *every time,* until students move quickly and efficiently from one lesson to another, minimizing the time off task. Dictatorial only at first, this method creates a consistent feeling of assurance.

Some teachers give 3- or 5-minute warnings about how much time children have to complete an activity. "We'll need to be finished with art projects in 5 minutes." Some teachers set a timer. "Three minutes, everyone." The most efficient of teachers, however, have coached their children to know exactly what is next on the schedule, so they are prepared and ready to move on.

Once you adopt a method of moving from one particular activity to another, stick with it. Such consistency on your part will not only create a comfort zone with children but also create *momentum,* a very desirable quality in a classroom. Momentum is the quality reflected in cases where the class seems to run itself, and students have been taught what to do when the period ends or the math lesson begins. The routine has been so reinforced that they "just do it." Smooth transitions occur because the rules are clear and the procedures have been established.

THE GOOD AND BAD SIDES OF PRAISE

Most people believe that we should look for good things about others for which we can praise them. And surely classroom teachers, of all people, should be in the habit of delivering positive comments. But effective teachers must be aware of the negative aspects of praise used with the misguided intention of building self-esteem or motivating children. Praise can undermine efforts to motivate if it's used inappropriately.

Some of us can recall being told in teacher training classes: "You must praise a child who does something good if you want him to keep acting that way." This common defense of praise, we now realize, implies that the only reason a child would ever demonstrate good behavior or an act of kindness was to be rewarded with the approval of an adult.

Praise may inspire some children to improve their behavior, and it may make them feel good for the moment, but there is a danger that praise will create dependence. These children may develop self-concepts that are totally dependent on the opinions of others, and others become their source of approval. When we tell some children how good they are, they light up, eager to please, and try to please us some more. These are the very children that may bring us concern.

Another example of a negative aspect of praise is when it is delivered by a teacher for the covert purpose of manipulation. Speaking within hearing of the whole class, her comment sounds like this: "I like the way Julie comes in quietly and gets right down to work." The teacher is actually *using* Julie, holding her up as an example in order to manipulate compliance from everyone else in the room. In this case the purpose of praise turns out to be a matter of benefiting the giver (the teacher) rather than the recipient. Making an example of someone to manipulate the behavior of others in the room is questionable at best.

PRAISE THE DEED, ENCOURAGE THE CHILD

For a more effective kind of praise, point out something that a student did well. "Brendan, your hard work on the experiment really paid off!" Express enthusiasm for what was accomplished. Give straightforward

Describe without evaluating. Report without judging.

information about how diligently a child is working on a task. "Kitty, I've watched you struggle with those math problems. Look at the progress you've made! Do you feel you've got it now?" Encourage the child to make her own judgments about what constitutes a good performance.

Give encouragement that leaves the recipient feeling a sense of determination. Point out an aspect of a drawing or story that is interesting, and allow this to be sufficient encouragement for new efforts. Remember, you aren't an art critic, but you can and should appreciate hard-won accomplishments.

Avoid praising people; praise what people do. And make it specific. Rather than saying, "You're such a good writer," say, "You've caught the mood of your characters." Rather than, "Oh, what a good painter you are," say, "You've given us several shades of blue in that scene." Focus your praise on individual improvement and never a comparison with the accomplishments of others.

Don't praise people, only what they do.

Converse with children in an authentic way. Respond genuinely and respectfully rather than giving pats-on-the-head comments or lavishing praise. Show your genuine delight. Be real.

Skillful teachers regularly use generous amounts of encouragement to inspire the behavior they want. Mrs. Presnall, a third-grade teacher, looks for opportunities to comment on acts of kindness or cooperation. As she walks toward the door with an armload of books, a student hurries to open the door and hold it for her. "Thanks, Carter," she says. "You got here just in time."

When a constant interrupter remembers to raise his hand with an answer, Mrs. Presnall comments on it. "Collin, I really appreciate it when you raise your hand." And later, when he starts to blurt out an answer, she quickly asks, "What do you do to be called on, Collin?" When he remembers, she thanks him again. Michelle Presnall knows that her encouragement increases the likelihood that cooperation will continue.

Focus on the art rather than the artist.

This teacher skillfully encourages academic improvement, keeping the focus on effort, not outcome. "You're getting better at that every day, Cody," she tells a struggling math student. "That hard work is really paying off!"

A parent arrives unexpectedly at her classroom door, causing Mrs. P. to step outside momentarily. The students recognize the chance to clown around, but they remain quiet at their work. "Thanks, guys," she says. "It's great to know I can count on you."

The problem with praise is that it makes people dependent on the approval of others.

All of the students in this teacher's class are being helped to make good choices because of her encouragement. They are learning to choose cooperation, improvement, responsibility, kindness to others, and good behavior. Encouraging messages are highly effective tools.

Offering Encouragement

1. That's the way to hang in there!

2. Nothing can stop you now!

3. Now you have the hang of it!

4. You've just about mastered that!

5. One more time and you'll have it!

6. You must have been practicing!

7. You're really working hard today!

8. Well, look at you now!

9. You're getting better every day!

10. It's a pleasure to teach you when you work so hard.

11. You're really learning a lot.

12. Now you've figured it out.

13. You haven't missed a thing!

14. I knew you could do it!

15. You've got that down pat!

16. You've got it made!

17. You're almost there!

18. You outdid yourself!

19. That's the way!

20. Good going!

21. Keep it up!

The Message Is:

Praise is tricky, and teachers should be aware of its negative repercussions. Praise is also very cheap and easy; no thought is required to make a nice comment. By contrast, it takes skill and care and attention to encourage people. Children need to know that they are so cared about that their teacher is willing to make the effort to offer specific, meaningful words of encouragement. Praise is easy; it takes skill to encourage!

NEGATIVE AND POSITIVE INTERVENTION

There will come the day when your best teaching fails. You do a beautiful job of presenting a lesson to the class, you lead group practice, and you allow them the opportunity to work on their own. Then, as you walk around, you notice that two or three are doing the work *wrong.*

When teachers are faced with this situation, the next few minutes are crucial. All too often, the teacher's response is to make a negative comment which places blame on the students instead of on the delivery of the lesson. Such negative comments, with a tone of exasperation, might be

- Okay. (sigh) Let's go over this *one more time!*
- Now *listen* this time while I explain, and this time *pay attention!*
- *Where were you* when I explained this?
- I *can't believe* you came up with this answer!

These are all unadorned failure messages, direct expressions of the teacher's frustration. Every message informs the students of their inadequacies.

A simple three-step intervention, suggested by Fred Jones, is more positive and preserves self-esteem. The three steps are: Praise, Prompt, and Leave.

- *Praise.* Tell the student what she has done right so far. ("This part is correct.")
- *Prompt.* Tell her what she should do next. ("Now, put a minus sign after the number.")

- *Leave.* Walk away, demonstrating faith in her ability to do the job correctly. (Don't stay to watch, but trust in the process.)

This three-step method is positive, quick, and never places blame. It praises what has been accomplished so far and offers encouragement to continue. It also allows you to move on to others who require help.

PARENTS MAKE A DIFFERENCE

Parents are their children's first and most influential teachers. Realizing this, wise teachers welcome their students' parents as partners. "Together we can make a difference" is their motto, for in a collaboration of teacher, parent, and student, the potential for success greatly increases.

We sometimes forget that parents want the same things for their children as we want. They want their children to be happy, to feel good about themselves, and to get along well with others. Most of all, they want their children to reach their full potential academically. So it is to our advantage as teachers to engage parents as partners.

Parents have important perspectives about their children, insights which we as teachers may not recognize. It is important to carefully solicit parents' perspectives on their child's strengths, interests, and habits as well as weaknesses and potential problems. This can be done at your first parent conference. Ask about the parents' expectations for their child's school year, and determine how and for what their child is disciplined at home. Listen attentively to this information, which will undoubtedly help you know each and every student. Jot this information down during the conference; it may come in handy at a later date.

Letters of welcome mailed home to parents were suggested in Chapter 2, and some teachers follow up such letters with a phone call to the parents of each child in their classroom. They let the parents know that their child's achievement is a cooperative effort between home and school, in which the child, parents, and teacher must work together. They mention that teachers often need help and support and hope the parents can be called on, if necessary.

Three times a year, Mr. Porter hosts a small parent meeting for all who'd like to come (adults only). He and the group sit in an informal circle to discuss any topic that comes up, perhaps common problems of children this age, or homework, or a certain area of the curriculum. There is only one rule for these meetings: No individual child may be discussed. Frank Porter believes that in this way he can build trust, credibility, and cooperation from home.

GUIDELINES TO SEND TO PARENTS

Parents appreciate seeing lists of discipline guidelines and reading improvement suggestions, along with the class rules which their children copied from the board. Suggest that they read them over with their student for complete understanding. The following is a sample list of guidelines and a parent letter which you can adapt to your situation:

1. Behave at all times in a mature, respectful, and responsible manner.

2. Be responsible for your schoolwork. Turn in quality work on time.

3. Be respectful toward your classmates, teachers, visitors, and school property.

4. Be reasonable in your expectations of others.

Letter to Parents

Dear Parents,

Each year concerned parents ask what they can do to encourage their children to learn to love books and therefore to love reading. Here are some reading guidelines developed by teacher-parent groups that have proven effective in promoting good attitudes toward reading and have resulted in increased reading skills.

1. Be a good model for your child. Visit the library and choose a book for yourself as well as for your child. Set aside time each day for quiet reading. Seeing you read each day will do more to encourage your child to read than repeated lectures. Try to discuss with your child some interesting aspects and favorite characters from your books.

2. Limit your child's television time! Do not be hesitant to enforce your role as parent in preventing your child from watching something that is not in his or her own interest.

3. Include some reading-out-loud time in your schedule. Encourage your child to read to you. Confidence can be strengthened by interest and encouragement! And no matter how old the child, you should still read aloud to him or her. Many of the children's classics can be equally enjoyable for child and parent.

4. An excellent way to encourage reluctant readers is to have them make their own books, complete with illustrations and a colorful cover. Typed pages give the book a more realistic appearance.

5. For birthday and holiday gifts, consider giving popular books or donating a book to the classroom or school library in your child's name.

6. Consult the librarian at your public school or school library about up-to-date book lists for various age groups. He or she will also be able to help you choose books on specific themes or interest levels.

7. Know what your child is doing at school so your home environment can reinforce the skills learned in the classroom.

_____
Teacher's signature

Copyright © 2005 by Corwin Press. All rights reserved. Reprinted from *Teach More and Discipline Less: Preventing Problem Behaviors in the K–6 Classroom,* by Barbara Reider. Thousand Oaks, CA: Corwin Press, www.corwinpress.com. Reproduction authorized only for the local school site that has purchased this book.

Occasionally you'll need parents to work cooperatively with you in correcting a student's misbehavior. As you contact the parents, keep in mind that they have seen copies of your class rules and discipline guidelines, and know what is expected. Remember, also, that they have a right and a responsibility to help and to reinforce the rules of the classroom.

Many teachers utilize a responsibility-building technique with a problem-solving plan. The child fills out the form at school, describing the problem as he sees it, the cause of the problem, and his ideas for a solution. Even young children can begin to recognize their responsibilities in causing and solving problems as they fill out this three-part form. A copy of the plan can be sent home with the child and mentioned in a phone call to elicit the parent's cooperation.

Problem-Solving Plan

1. The problem as I see it: _____

   _____

2. The causes of this problem: _____

   _____

3. My plan to solve this problem: _____

   _____

   _____
   Student's signature

   _____
   Date

Copyright © 2005 by Corwin Press. All rights reserved. Reprinted from *Teach More and Discipline Less: Preventing Problem Behaviors in the K–6 Classroom*, by Barbara Reider. Thousand Oaks, CA: Corwin Press, www.corwinpress.com. Reproduction authorized only for the local school site that has purchased this book.

The Message Is:

When school and home environments reinforce one another, learning is likely to increase and behavior problems decrease.

Parents are the original teachers.

Figure 5.3 Parent volunteers are indispensable in a class of young writers.

Working together we make a difference.

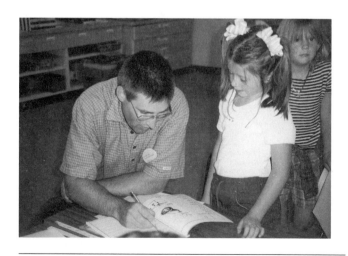

Figure 5.4 This dad spends one hour a week in his daughter's classroom.

UNIQUE TECHNIQUES

Modeling

Model the values and behaviors you want to see in students. If you are well organized and in control, you provide examples for your students by your behavior. As we all know, values are caught, not taught.

If you want children to read with expression, overemphasize the characters' voices when you read aloud. Be a ham! Exclaim with excitement at thrilling episodes, and "sneak up" on a mystery. Let your voice show disgust and anguish, anticipation and surprise and wonder!

If you wish your students to be more courteous, constantly model courtesy in small everyday comments. Say, "Feel free to ask me if you need help." "Blue is a nice color on you." "Thank you for sharing your feelings."

Monitoring

After you have given a deskwork assignment and students have begun to work, go to the back of the room and sit down. Wait quietly for a minute or two, then make a pass through the classroom. Check to see if names are on papers, that everyone has begun working, and that all have understood the assignment. Provide individualized help where needed.

This technique is very effective. You'll get the slow-pokes working and startle the dreamers into action. Two minutes will do it.

Name Dropping

If you notice a student talking or otherwise not paying attention, try a subtle technique, called name dropping, adopted by clever teachers. Noticing that one of your boys is daydreaming while you explain a math process at the board, you drop in his name in an offhand way: "And you see, Zachary, we carry the 1 to the 10's column." Zachary is startled to hear his name and gets back to work. Others in the class are not distracted.

Time to Line Up

Occasionally you have a little extra time just before kids line up. For the fun of it, try one of these ways to get kids in a row.

Line Up If You Can Tell Me

1. The name of a television character

2. The name of a city: New York, London, . . .

3. The name of a country: Scotland, India, . . .

4. A book title (or author, or character)

5. A kind of fruit

6. A kind of vegetable

7. A type of tree

8. A type of flower

9. An animal that lives in the zoo

10. An animal on a farm

Line Up If You Have

1. A tooth missing

2. A t-shirt on (long sleeves or shorts)

3. A ribbon in your hair (a watch on your arm)

4. A "z" in your name ("p," "q," . . .)

5. A birthday in January, February, etc.

6. A pet dog (or cat, bird, fish)

7. Striped socks on (white socks, no socks)

8. Flown in an airplane (air balloon, helicopter)

9. Helped parents mow grass (wash car, plant garden)

10. Moved to a new town (state, country)

11. Blue eyes, brown eyes, gray eyes

12. Been to a hospital for tonsils (broken bones)

Signals and Directions

Eye Contact

- Keep your eyes moving; scan the entire room every 30 seconds.
- Avert potential classroom misbehaviors through timely eye contact.
- Add an occasional wink at times, or a frown when appropriate.

Kid Signals for Whole-Class Response

- Thumbs up = Yes
- Thumbs down = No
- Thumb and little finger sideways = No Opinion

RX: TAKE ONE SPONGE WHEN NEEDED

Sponges are classroom management tools used to create a smoothly flowing instructional day. They get their name from their ability to "soak up" time. Sponges help with transitions, or those spaces of time between lessons, or when work is done. Use a sponge when individual students finish their work at varying times, or when the class lesson has ended 5 or 10 minutes before the bell. It is very handy to have all of these sponge activities printed on 10 × 10-inch signs. Display one a day, or one a week, as you wish.

Sponge Activities

New inventions are created every day. Design a new piece of equipment for our playground.

Tell how you would persuade someone that this month is the best month of the year.

Predict: Would more people in our classroom choose a computer or a robot? Why?

Choose your favorite place to read a book. Give reasons for your choice.

Choose a present you would like to give to our school. Give the reasons for your choice.

Invent a new kind of soup. Tell why people would like to eat this kind of soup.

Charles Perrault was best known for his book of fairy tales. Choose another ending for the story "Cinderella."

Everyone likes nicknames. Choose a nickname for yourself, and give the reason for your choice.

Decide all the things you and your family should consider before adopting a dog.

List all the advantages and disadvantages of having your computer programmed to do all your work.

Imagine you are a parent in our class. Decide things you would like to hear about your child.

Choose words to complete this recipe for a happy day:
1 cup _____, 2 cups _____,
1 spoonful _____.

List all of the things you believe will bring you good luck.

Imagine you are in a hot air balloon. Decide where you would like the balloon to take you, and tell why.

Invent a new way to build a snowman, or a ski run, without using snow.

List the reasons why children should or should not be allowed to travel in space.

(Continued)

(Continued)

Imagine that you hibernated all winter. Decide the first five things you would do upon waking up.	Write your three new ideas for making our school better.
Compose questions that can be answered with the word Spring (also Summer, Winter).	Leprechauns wanted! Decide the qualifications needed to be a leprechaun.
Today our class has no paper. Decide how we will spend our time without any paper.	School Secretary wanted! Decide the qualifications needed to be a good school secretary.
We honor mothers on a day in May. Decide the qualifications needed to be a good mom.	Design a medal for your mother. Tell why she would be given this medal.
Imagine you are at the beach this summer and find a bottle floating in the water. Decide what the message in the bottle says.	Imagine our school has been put up for sale. Decide how you would describe our school in the newspaper ad.
Imagine you have the power to select a new principal for just one day. Who will it be, and what are your reasons?	Imagine that you planted seeds in your garden. Decide all the things that will be growing in your garden.
Imagine that your pet could talk. What would you ask your pet, and what would your pet ask you?	List the advantages and disadvantages of having telephones that allow us to see the person with whom we are talking.
People in England believe that ashes from a Yule log bring good luck. List the things that you believe will bring you good luck.	Newspapers have been published for hundreds of years. Decide what headlines about our school you would like to read in the newspaper.
Predict which one of our classroom rules the principal will think is most important. Give your reason.	Thomas Edison invented the first electric lamp in 1879. List all the things in your home that need electricity to work.

"MY BEST TEACHER"

Once in a while it's good to ask students what qualities make a good teacher. As teachers we often ask colleagues for feedback and we read helpful books written by educators, but rarely do we ask children for their opinions about us. Perhaps we could learn what it takes to be an exemplary teacher by asking students. Here are a few answers from the mouths of 11- and 12-year-olds.

- "She's excited about what she teaches. You can tell she really likes it."
- "He presents ordinary stuff in an interesting way."
- "She knows when to be strict. Only when it's really necessary."
- "He thinks it is okay to, like, really laugh."
- "He teaches in a fun way so that it will stick."
- "He talks to us like we're real people, not just children."
- "Our feelings are more important than rules."

ROUNDUP OF CHAPTER 5

1. Concentrate on asking higher-level questions to challenge thinking.

2. Build your questioning skills, taking special care to be nonjudgmental about children's responses.

3. Carefully teach and practice transition procedures.

4. Be aware of the negative connotations of praise.

5. Praise not the child but what he does; encourage self-determination.

6. Master the techniques of giving messages of encouragement.

7. Try the Praise, Prompt, and Leave method of individual help.

8. Build a partnership with parents.

9. Remember to keep parents informed about rules and expectations.

10. Model the behaviors you want children to "catch."

11. Try some clever ways to line up your class.

12. Use sponge activities to fill in the gaps.

6 Respond to Misbehavior

A FEW INEVITABLE BEHAVIOR PROBLEMS

In the five previous chapters you have considered how teachers build their fences, circle their wagons, and get their ponies in a row. However, you are well aware that in many classes some of the wild ponies won't cooperate! It seems to be true that whenever we corral 20 or 30 energetic, imaginative young people within four walls and begin to give them instructions, a few of them decide to test the boundaries. It also seems that as soon as these young people recognize that the adult in charge has an agenda which they may not like, they begin to provide a few discipline challenges. Let's face it: They act up!

Hopefully you are ready for them. Hopefully rules and procedures have been established and a sense of community has been promoted. Hopefully a feeling of class pride is constantly encouraged, and building self-esteem is a top priority.

The best teachers spend very little time dealing with student misbehavior; not that they ignore it, but they have developed strategies and created an environment for preventing problems in the first place. Behavioral infractions are less frequent and less severe, and when they do occur, it is less difficult to recapture students' attention and get them back on task. The best teachers just don't worry about discipline.

However, it is worthwhile to look at methods of responding to those few behavior problems that seem to be inevitable in every class. In this chapter we will consider methods to solve problems in ways that reduce their recurrence and help children make better choices. Included are some methods that don't work, such as the use of punishment and rewards, and many methods that have been proven successful.

Suppose a student does something hurtful or mean. Immediately you, the teacher, make a choice about how to handle the problem. According to the educator Alfie Kohn, you will choose between two options: (1) You decide, "This child has done something bad, now something bad must be done to him." (2) Or you say, "We have a problem here; how are we going to solve it?" Unfortunately, some of us are accustomed to choosing the first option, which is easier and less time-consuming, but not in the best interests of the child.

In this chapter we will look at techniques and strategies that support Option 2, using a democratic approach to respond to misbehavior. It takes courage not to punish and time and effort to respond constructively to misbehavior.

STOP A PROBLEM BEFORE IT HAPPENS

Scrutinize your students carefully to discover which of them may be potential behavior problems, and then take the time to build a special one-to-one relationship with each of these children. Talk to them on the playground. Make time during lunch to strike up a conversation. Find out who they are, what they believe, and what they like and don't like about school. Discover what you can about problems they might have had in previous school years.

Whenever a potential misbehaver does something *right*, offer him reinforcing encouragement: "You made a good decision." When you catch him following a rule, staying on task, or avoiding an argument, tell him, "Good job. You could have made a bad choice there, but you used your head." Offer this reinforcement in private whenever possible.

You are building a relationship that will prove essential for you when problems occur. It is far easier to resolve a conflict with a student when the two of you have a caring relationship on which to build, especially if the child has done something wrong and feels angry or defensive. From a child's standpoint, no problem-solving strategy, regardless of how clever or well-meaning, can take the place of the feeling of being accepted and cared for by the teacher.

Problem Prevention Strategies: A Checklist

_____ I consistently reinforce standard procedures.

_____ My classroom procedures are now routine.

_____ I carefully calculate my seating arrangement.

_____ I use a calm, quiet tone of voice.

_____ I consistently enforce the class-made rules.

_____ I spend time planning and organizing.

_____ I make it a point to know each of my students.

_____ I look carefully at the self-esteem of each child.

_____ I have established a comfortable class environment.

_____ I promote ownership of the classroom.

_____ I promote a sense of class pride.

_____ I respect varied opinions.

_____ I maintain a sense of humor.

_____ I promote a feeling of community within the classroom.

_____ I conduct frequent class discussions.

_____ I carefully teach and practice transition procedures.

_____ I build partnerships with parents.

_____ I involve my class in problem-solving procedures.

_____ I build a one-to-one relationship with potential misbehavers.

Copyright © 2005 by Corwin Press. All rights reserved. Reprinted from _Teach More and Discipline Less: Preventing Problem Behaviors in the K-6 Classroom_ by Barbara Reider. Thousand Oaks, CA: Corwin Press, www.corwinpress.com. Reproduction authorized only for the local school site that has purchased this book.

A POSITIVE LOOK AT MISBEHAVIOR

Effective teachers train themselves to notice and reinforce positive behavior. With practice, they seek out small acts of cooperation, instances of tolerance and responsibility, and observance of class rules. Although it is easy to do just the opposite, these teachers behave as though they have a sign on their desks saying, "Catch kids doing something good." Their response to good behavior is to offer positive reinforcement and encouragement. As we have seen in previous chapters, these teachers constantly build a caring class climate.

Methods of acknowledging and reinforcing appropriate behavior go hand in hand with techniques for dealing with misbehavior. Strategies to be discussed in this chapter include employing a "teacher look," setting limits, and following up with logical consequences. All promote discipline with encouragement and kind words rather than rebukes or reprimands.

Research tells us that sarcasm, ridicule, and other means of punishment are ineffective at best and hurtful at worst. Good teachers generally agree with the following statements about punishment.

The Deadly Effects of Punishment

1. Punishment is intended to change a child's behavior.

2. Punishment is deliberately chosen to be unpleasant.

3. Punishment makes somebody suffer in order to teach a lesson.

4. Teachers sometimes give bad grades as punishment.

5. Privileges are taken away in order to punish.

6. Humiliation is frequently used to punish.

7. Children may be sent to the principal as punishment.

8. Detention is occasionally the chosen punishment.

9. Punishment may take the form of extra work.

10. Longer assignments in school teach children that learning is repugnant.

---

11. Punishment by physical force teaches that aggression is acceptable.

12. Punishment models the use of power.

13. Children learn to make something bad happen to another child until he gives in.

14. Students learn to avoid the adult who is the enforcer.

15. Punishment means upset and burn-out for the adult, but it also means rejection and alienation for the child.

16. Punishment can drive a wedge between teacher and child that will ultimately destroy the child's motivation to cooperate.

17. Punishment fails to solve problems.

18. Punishment frequently makes problems worse.

19. When a child is punished he resolves to be more wary, not more honest and responsible.

20. At best, punishment elicits only temporary compliance.

TEMPORARY COMPLIANCE

If you ask teachers if they ever rely on punishment, many will answer yes. I know, I've asked them. And many of their replies sound, on the surface, reasonable. They say, "If you don't give some kind of punishment, kids think they can get away with it." Or they say, "It takes a lot of time and effort to reason with a kid; this is quick and easy." They say, "It handles the problem, at least temporarily, so I can get on with teaching the rest of the class."

Most teachers mean well. Reasoning *does* take time, and the education of the other 27 students *is* important. Moreover, if the misbehavior stops even temporarily because of punishment, teachers are often fooled into thinking it works. Teachers need to remember that, in the long run, punishment fails. Children may comply out of fear of getting into trouble, or because they are rewarded, but when punished, *never* are they motivated to behave properly nor to become people who think for themselves and care about others.

There has to be a better way of responding to misbehavior.

If I misbehave, will you notice me?

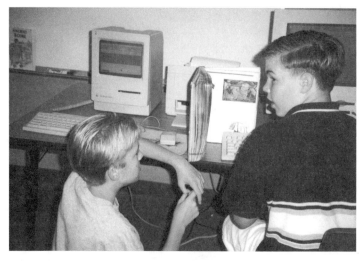

Figure 6.1   Expect responsible behavior in all activities.

THE "TEACHER LOOK" FOR SMALL VIOLATIONS

Every teacher should master the "teacher look" before he or she receives a credential! This is the response to be used for the "small stuff"— the less serious offenses that students commit but cannot be ignored. Perhaps you'll need to stand before a mirror and practice this indispensable technique; it is an art that experienced teachers have rehearsed to perfection!

Be consistent! Never respond one time and ignore the next.

The teacher look is stern, accompanied by a slight frown that stares the offender in the eye. It is silent and unwavering. It says without words, "Your classmates and I do not appreciate this disturbance. You are making a bad choice." The look may last between two to five beats, or until it has had the desired effect.

Never debate with a student, or allow yourself to be drawn into a verbal dispute. Absolute silence will give a student no chance to manipulate you. Good teachers do not show they are upset; they stay cool, calm, and collected because they know that calm is strength and upset portrays weakness. They *will* themselves to relax, take a deep breath, and keep their composure.

If your teacher look doesn't seem to have the desired effect, slowly walk toward the misbehaver's desk. Continue teaching the lesson unperturbed. If necessary, rest a hand on his desk, or even lean on it, without directing attention toward him. Take great care not to break the momentum of your instruction.

Many unseasoned teachers are ambivalent about discipline management. They want to mean business, but they also want the students to like them. Learn to maintain a balance in the attitude you display. Ambivalence will send a mixed message to the students: You want them to know, without a doubt, that you are in charge.

Calmness is the key. The teacher look is one simple but very useful technique.

Teacher Note

Keep in mind the popular adage, "Don't sweat the small stuff." And just as important, train yourself to distinguish the small stuff from more serious misbehavior. The teacher look is essential for small stuff.

Calm is strength. Upset is weakness.

Figure 6.2   A teacher look requires no words.

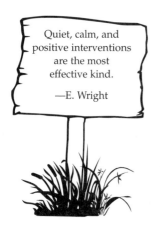

Quiet, calm, and positive interventions are the most effective kind.

—E. Wright

Figure 6.3   Kids can take a deep breath and consider one of these suggestions.

THE DEMOCRATIC APPROACH TO MISBEHAVIOR

Part 1: Setting Clear Limits

Mrs. Shroeder adheres to a democratic approach to misbehavior in her second-grade classroom.

She began setting clear limits during the first weeks of school by introducing her standard procedures; therefore, her students know beyond a shadow of a doubt precisely when they may visit with neighbors and where and when to turn in their homework. They are undeniably aware that the consequence for work left unfinished is to lose the privileges of a Fun Friday Afternoon. In addition, the class created a list of rules for classroom conduct, so her students are very clear about their decision to do their best work and be respectful toward others.

This wise teacher followed Part 1 of the democratic approach by giving her students the information they needed to make acceptable choices about their behavior. They now have the freedom to choose to follow the rules and procedures, or to disregard them. Next they need to know what will happen if they misbehave, so Mrs. Shroeder will follow through with Part 2, the consequences for misbehavior, when the occasion arises.

Jerry and Antonio, two second graders, have decided to ignore the rules during math period. They are supposedly working on a collaborative project in a small group, but they find that flicking math manipulatives at each other is much more fun. Soon one of the group members complains to the teacher. "Mrs. Shroeder, these boys are playing around and not doing their part."

Mrs. Shroeder turns toward Jerry and Antonio with her most stern teacher look. Walking their way, she observes as Antonio goes back to his work, but as she turns her back, another missile flies through the air and lands at her feet. Obviously, her stern look was only partially effective. "Jerry," she says quietly, "I expect you to help your group with this project. Would you prefer to do the work here, or at your desk?" "I'll stay here," says Jerry.

The teacher walks away, but within 5 minutes Jerry is again disrupting the group. "Take your work to your desk, Jerry. You have chosen to work alone," she says. Jerry retreats to his desk; the incident is over. It has been handled skillfully, respectfully, and fairly by Mrs. Shroeder, a wise teacher who used a "teacher look," offered the offender a choice, and then followed through by delivering a logical consequence.

Part 2: Following Through With Consequences

The students in the class described above have been reminded that behavior is a choice. Many try to blame someone else for their misbehavior (including their mothers!), but they are coming to understand that no one makes them do anything. Rather they make their own choices. They also need to know that they alone control the consequences of their behavior.

Consequences are the second part of a limit-setting message. "Consequences speak louder than words," declares Robert MacKenzie, author of *Setting Limits in the Classroom*, a highly recommended book. Along with a majority of experienced educators, he would agree that consequences

- Stop behavior
- Provide clear answers to children's questions about what's acceptable
- Teach responsibility
- Hold children accountable for their choices and behavior
- Define the path you want your students to stay on

The best consequences are reasonable and logical; that is, they follow logically from the behavior and are not arbitrarily imposed. If a student turns in a messy paper, the logical consequence is for him to redo the paper. If a child persists in annoying others, the logical consequence is for him to move his desk 6 feet away from other students. Other examples of consequences are loss of a privilege such as recess or free time, or being last in line for lunch.

Many teachers use a discipline technique called "time out" as a consequence for disrupting the class. This strategy, also referred to as "thinking time," allows the class to continue work undisturbed while the disruptive student has a chance to cool down and reflect, away from the group. It is advisable to place a "time out chair" where it can be seen by the teacher, but is out of view of other students. Time in "time out" should be limited to no longer than 10 minutes. It is also beneficial to require that the child write responses to these statements: (1) Why I am in time out. (2) What I will do to correct my behavior.

> **Teacher Note**
>
> By applying consequences in a democratic manner you can stop misbehavior and reinforce rules and procedures in the clearest and most effective way.

The Message Is:

The democratic style of teaching is respectful, instructive, and fair. Not only does it teach responsibility, but it deters misbehavior.

Tips for a Democratic Approach to Behavior

1. Remain calm when addressing a child's misbehavior.
2. Take a deep breath and speak in a positive tone.
3. Always be considerate of a child's feelings.
4. Make sure a child understands the infraction.
5. Avoid a reprimand in public.
6. If a reprimand is necessary, state it quickly.
7. Never reprimand in the heat of the moment.
8. Focus on the desired behavior rather than the mistake. "Please walk," rather than "Don't run."
9. Give the student a choice. (Do your work now or during recess.)
10. Schedule a private discussion after class.
11. Avoid consequences that are related to a student's grades.
12. Be sure that students realize that consequences are the result of choices.
13. Have high expectations that all rules will be followed.
14. Let each student start each day with a clean slate.
15. Be consistent and fair with every child.
16. Admit your mistakes. Apologize if necessary.
17. Focus on recognizing acceptable behavior.

WHEN "NO" MEANS "MAYBE"

Much has been said throughout this book about standard procedures and the importance that they be consistently upheld. These procedures, along with class rules, serve as clear limits for behavior. Indeed, limits convey our classroom expectations.

However, problems arise when limits are unclear or when compliance is optional; when "no" means "maybe" or "sometimes." Sadly this is a problem more common than we'd like to admit, one that sharply reminds us what happens when procedures are not effectively taught and maintained. The following is an example of a procedure maintained ineffectively.

Kenny is well aware of the procedure for doing work without talking, but Kenny likes to clown around. Every day he finds something funny with which to entertain his neighbors. Mrs. Hadley, however, keeps trying to ignore his behavior in hopes it'll go away. Kenny continues his whispered jokes.

Finally his teacher has heard enough, so she begins to lecture Kenny at length. "The class doesn't think you're funny, Kenneth," she says. "And I don't appreciate all this clowning around. Now everybody will be finished with the class work and you'll be the last one done. Do you want to miss recess? It would be a shame if I have to mention this behavior to the principal. What would it be like if everyone behaved this way? Now I want you to settle down." Mrs. Hadley sermonizes ad infinitum.

Has Kenny learned anything constructive from this teacher's method of handling his misbehavior? Will he stop entertaining his classmates? The answer to both questions is no. If anything, Kenny has learned that this teacher will ignore the misbehavior for a considerable length of time, and then will deliver a lengthy lecture that he can easily ignore. Moreover, the other students have discovered that compliance to rules and procedures is optional in this class. Mrs. Hadley's approach is sadly ineffectual.

Some teachers give untold numbers of second chances and numerous warnings to "stop that mischief right now!" Some resort to repeating directions and giving reminders while students continue to misbehave, pushing an inch to a mile. Other misinformed teachers argue, plead, cajole, bargain, negotiate, and offer bribes. These teachers are delivering the message that it's okay to ignore and tune them out. In few cases are they deterring children's misbehavior.

Robert MacKenzie offers clear suggestions for teachers who wish to mean *No* when they say *No*. To improve the quality of verbal messages he advises

1. Be direct and specific.

2. Specify your consequences.

3. Support your words with effective action.

4. Be prepared to follow through.

Unclear Limits

- Do not require compliance
- Don't convey teacher's expectations
- Are not regularly followed
- Allow students to test boundaries
- Promote misbehavior and power struggles
- Teach students that adults don't mean what they say
- Bring confusion and failure for students
- Cause frustration on the part of the teacher

Clear Limits

- Are stated clearly and reviewed regularly
- Require cooperation and compliance
- Bring a clear understanding of expectations
- Result in teacher-student accord
- Ensure that teachers' words are taken seriously
- Are encouraging and instructional
- Lead to a smoothly run classroom

THE DOWNSIDE OF REWARDS

Studies confirm that rewards are used in many schools across America in the attempt to motivate students and manage classrooms. Students are offered stickers and stars, candy, treats, and extra recesses, and as they get older they are rewarded with silver and gold I.D. cards.

Reward systems are all subtle variations of efforts to control. When we offer students special rewards in return for cooperation, good work, and acceptable behavior, aren't we really saying with our actions that we don't expect these results unless we pay them off?

Consider these messages regarding handing out rewards.

Rewards: Short-Time Solutions

1. Giving a reward, like giving punishment, is a method of control.

2. "Do this and you'll get that" is the message behind both punishment and rewards.

3. Rewards control by seduction.

4. Rewards can make children dependent on the approval of others.

5. Rewards cause kids to believe "I'm okay if others say I'm okay."

6. To induce students to behave, some are rewarded with popcorn and video parties.

7. To induce students to learn, some are presented with stickers and certificates.

8. Some parents reward high grades with money or toys.

9. Typically, it is assumed that rewards will increase interest in learning and improve behavior.

10. The whole point of giving rewards is to manipulate students' behavior.

11. Rewards promote a "what's in it for me?" attitude.

12. Rewards induce compliance, but never make long-lasting changes.

13. Rewards, like punishments, are useless in helping children become careful thinkers and self-directed learners.

14. Children soon realize that rewards are used for controlling.

15. Doing something for a reward makes students less truly interested in what they are doing.

16. Rewards motivate people merely to get rewards.

The preceding statements point out the ever-present danger that rewards can cause a negative change in a child's motivation for learning. Melissa, who had been learning happily and naturally in Kindergarten, is now given a sticker in first grade whenever she adds up a row of numbers. As a result she now strives for extrinsic rewards rather than intrinsic reinforcers such as the joy of a job well done. Melissa finds that she can earn

"Eagle Awards" for picking up trash on the school grounds or for helping a small child find the bathroom, both deeds that she did anyway before her teacher began giving out rewards.

As teachers, we must raise our sights beyond rewarding children in school. We need to take a close look at any program that hands out rewards for cooperation and good behavior. These are things we should expect children to do and children should do for intrinsic reasons.

The best reward: The satisfaction of a job well done.

Figure 6.4   Engrossed in an intricate project.

The Message Is:

Young children don't need to be rewarded to learn. The desire to learn is natural. As children get older they will remain optimal learners as long as they are *interested* in what they are learning. When they have a learning environment in which they don't feel controlled, students generally look forward to the challenges of learning. *We* set up the environment. *We* create the climate.

BEYOND PRAISE AND REWARDS

In his book, *Inspiring Active Learning*, Merrill Harmon warns us against the undesirable effects of most praise and rewards. He cautions that it can become addictive, "providing immediate, easy, and superficial satisfaction while smothering our self-motivation and initiative."

Frequently, overblown praise and rewards are given to certain students while others seem to receive far less praise. Such unfairness leads some to conclude that not everyone in the class is worthy. However, skillful teachers can support and encourage students without inviting harmful side effects, by using techniques such as the following:

1. Give specific appreciation.
   - "I like the way you said that."
   - "That's the way to give it a try."

2. Offer empathetic acceptance.
   - "I've often made that same mistake."
   - "Lots of us here can understand how you feel."

3. Give a kindly look that communicates your full attention.

4. Give a bit of your extra time.

5. Provide a little private instruction or guidance.

6. Show concern over a flushed face or a tired look.

7. Offer simple confirmation rather than overblown praise.
   - "Yes, that's right."
   - "Just what I wanted."

8. Offer a simple correction.
   - "You had it partly right. The answer is after the Civil War."
   - "That's the answer for the Ohio River. The correct answer is St. Louis."

9. Give praise to the entire group.
   - "Give yourselves a hand for some very difficult work."
   - "You're really a powerful bunch today."

10. Appreciate values you wish to encourage.
    - "I like the way you defended your friend."
    - "Nice time plan you've drawn up."

THREE WORKABLE SYSTEMS

Although it has been proven that reward systems do not make long-lasting changes, they do induce temporary compliance, and it is for this reason that some teachers use them. As a teacher, you will make a personal decision as to their use in your classroom. Therefore, a few of the least obtrusive systems are described here.

1. Marble Jar

In the marble jar system the teacher keeps a supply of marbles within easy reach so she can drop one into the marble jar each time the class enters the room quietly or works industriously at assignments. When the jar is full of marbles the class is rewarded with a movie on video or a popcorn party. This system is unobtrusive in that students hear the marble drop, smile, and continue working.

2. Card Chart

Some teachers set up a pocket chart using library card pockets displayed on the wall, with students' names on the pockets. Four colored cards are placed in each pocket (gold, orange, red, and blue in a specific order).

When the fourth graders enter Mrs. McClurg's classroom each morning, only gold cards are showing (chosen because their class motto is "Go for the Gold.") Should a child misbehave, he must place his gold card behind the others, revealing an orange card. Any child with an orange card will spend 5 minutes of his recess writing a letter of explanation, including a list of the class rules. Should his card be changed to red that day, he would be required to take the letter home for a parent signature. A blue card would designate a referral to the principal's office.

Conducting a card chart system is popular with teachers because it is unobtrusive and very visual. No verbal reminders are necessary. When a child chooses to misbehave the teacher merely asks him to go to the chart and change his card.

3. Five-Minute List

Mr. Douglas keeps a clipboard handy with a "Five-Minute List," which is always available for any student to read. On it he writes the name of anyone who chooses to disturb others, blurt out comments, waste time, or fail to follow directions. Any student whose name appears on the list has thereby chosen to spend 5 minutes of his recess at his desk with his head down. On Friday, Mr. Douglas gives a Super Behavior Award to all those whose names have not appeared on the list that week.

In the
long run,
punishment
fails.

Figure 6.5   A card chart is unobtrusive in that it
requires no verbal reprimands.

Acceptable rewards:
- Smiles
- Pats on the back
- Thank you's
- High fives
- A note sent home
- A phone call to parents

Figure 6.6   Children choose what to display on their
own section of wall.

Responses That Backfire

The following is a list of techniques that do not work. Many of them were gathered by Linda Albert, author of *Cooperative Discipline*, who surveyed dozens of teachers, asking them what methods backfired for them.

- Raising my voice
- Saying, "I'm the boss here"
- Insisting on having the last word
- Using degrading, insulting, or embarrassing put-downs
- Using sarcasm
- Attacking the student's character
- Acting superior
- Insisting that I am right
- Preaching
- Backing the student into a corner
- Pleading or bribing
- Making unsubstantiated accusations
- Holding a grudge
- Making comparisons with siblings
- Giving rewards

MOTIVATING STUDENTS TO LEARN

Jean Johnson, a highly-skilled teacher who is also a speaker at teacher conferences, admits that teaching teachers how to motivate children is a difficult task. Yet she receives frequent requests to speak on the topic of motivation. "Children learn when they have a reason," Mrs. Johnson states, "and teachers must be there to help them find their reasons."

There are two types of motivation: external and internal. When children expect rewards for good behavior or for completing their work, they are said to be externally motivated. External, or extrinsic, motivators include extra privileges, stars and stickers, candy and treats, and most kinds of praise. Internal, or intrinsic, motivation, on the other hand, is fueled by the joy of learning for learning's sake.

Children are born with intrinsic motivation, a quality as basic as breathing. They are naturally curious and naturally eager to learn. As they grow older, these students approach tasks seriously, carry them out carefully, and believe they will benefit from them. Children who are intrinsically motivated work to gain a sense of accomplishment and a sense of mastery, a feeling of success and a sense of ownership. They often work just for the satisfaction of curiosity or for knowledge for its own sake.

When I asked a wise sixth-grade teacher how she rewards her students, she replied, "With a smile. With a compliment in private. With a fond look that says 'I appreciate you.' Perhaps with a positive phone call home to the parents." Other wise teachers hold popcorn parties, not as rewards but just because it's snowing outside, or it's the first day of spring. To keep students intrinsically motivated, a teacher can

- Take into account their individual styles and preferences
- Promote questioning and seeking answers
- Let them select their own topics
- Communicate a belief that learning is fun, exciting, and personally meaningful
- Present difficult lessons in a positive way
- Design activities to capitalize on student interests
- Enthusiastically express his or her own personal interests or experiences
- Select activities that are relevant and fun

Why reward a positive response with tangible prizes? Let's instead help children find the inner rewards of learning, cooperating, and helping others.

EXCELLENCE IN TEACHING

Over the years all of us have known people whom we call "natural teachers." They seem never to raise their voices or get upset. They also seem to rarely have discipline problems, and all of their students appear content. Author Fred Jones describes the approach used by natural teachers as "a process of training the class to follow rules out of habit and a genuine desire to cooperate." They rely on their own inner qualities of love, integrity, and commitment.

We all notice the self-assuredness of natural teachers, communicated by quiet composure and conscious eye contact. In the classroom they use their voices for control, speaking softly so that everyone becomes quiet in order to hear. They are gentle yet powerful in that they calmly demand courtesy in exchange for the courtesy they give. As these teachers move around the room visiting areas of potential trouble, they have high expectations. They present an appropriate level of challenge in their lessons, and they expect their students to work diligently and behave appropriately. And their students do.

Excellent teachers are consistent in every way. Students can depend on them to be pleasant in the morning, tolerant of their mistakes, and receptive to their questions. But on the other hand, students know these teachers will be equally consistent in an absolute intolerance of misbehavior. No one will be allowed to disregard rules that the class has established. The students feel a sense of safety and assurance that everyone in their classroom will be treated fairly and with respect.

Much thought and planning goes into their teaching, yet the best teachers remain flexibly open for spontaneous discovery as opportunities arise. They genuinely believe in the value of their subject matter; they're enthusiastic, even passionate, about what they teach. These excellent teachers are likely to incorporate a variety of strategies into their programs. They possess a broad repertoire of teaching skills, and they constantly try to upgrade their knowledge.

The best teachers are persons who are not only clever and insightful but "with it" and fun to be around. They are special people who have chosen to spend their lives in the most important profession in the world.

ROUNDUP OF CHAPTER 6

1. Build a special one-to-one relationship with potential misbehavers.

2. Check your problem-prevention strategies.

3. Consistently reinforce good behavior.

4. Avoid the deadly effects of punishment.

5. Remind students that they *choose* their behavior.

6. Perfect your "teacher look" to use for small offenses.

7. Remember the power of being calm and collected.

8. Never let yourself be drawn into a verbal dispute.

9. Adopt a democratic approach to handling behavior problems.

10. Tender clear limits and logical consequences.

11. Avoid the countereffects of giving tangible rewards.

12. Develop alternative ways to appreciate and encourage.

13. Keep in mind the two types of motivation: external and internal.

14. Find "natural teachers" to emulate.

15. Become a model of excellence in your chosen profession.

References and Suggested Readings

Albert, Linda. (1989). *Cooperative discipline.* Circle Pines, MN: American Guidance Service, Inc.

Gibbs, Jeanne (1987). *Tribes.* Santa Rosa, CA: Center Source Publications.

Ginott, Haim (1972). *Teacher and child.* New York: Avon Books.

Glasser, William (1969). *Schools without failure.* New York: Harper & Row.

Harmon, Merrill (1994). *Inspiring active learning.* Alexandria, VA: ASCD.

Jones, Fred (1987). *Positive classroom discipline.* New York: McGraw-Hill.

Kohn, Alfie (1993). *Punished by rewards.* New York: Houghton Mifflin.

Kohn, Alfie (1996). *Beyond discipline.* Alexandria, VA: ASCD.

MacKenzie, Robert (1996). *Setting limits in the classroom.* Rocklin, CA: Prima Publishing.

Nelsen, Jane (1981). *Positive discipline.* Fair Oaks, CA: Sunrise Press.

Nelsen, J., Lott, L., & Glenn, S. (1993). *Positive discipline in the classroom.* Rocklin, CA: Prima Publishing.

Partin, Ronald (1995). *Classroom teacher's survival guide.* West Nyack, NY: Center for Applied Research in Education.

Reider, Barbara (1993). *Notes in the lunchbox . . . How to help your child succeed at school.* El Dorado Hills, CA: Sierra House Publishing.

Reider, Barbara (1998). *A hooray kind of kid . . . A child's self-esteem and how to build it.* El Dorado Hills, CA: Sierra House Publishing.

Shalaway, Linda (1997). *Learning to teach.* New York: Scholastic Professional Books.

Wong, Harry & Wong, Rosemary (1991). *The first days of school.* Sunnyvale, CA: Harry K. Wong Publications.

Wright, Esther (1994). *Loving discipline.* San Francisco, CA: Teaching From the Heart.

Wright, Esther (1989). *Good morning class. I love you!* Rolling Hills Estates, CA: Jalmar Press.

Index

**CORWIN
PRESS**

The Corwin Press logo—a raven striding across an open book—represents the union of courage and learning. Corwin Press is committed to improving education for all learners by publishing books and other professional development resources for those serving the field of K–12 education. By providing practical, hands-on materials, Corwin Press continues to carry out the promise of its motto: **"Helping Educators Do Their Work Better."**